CONNECT

Smyth & Helwys Publishing, Inc.
6316 Peake Road
Macon, Georgia 31210-3960
1-800-747-3016

The paper used in this publication meets the minimum requirements of
American National Standard for Information Sciences—
Permanence of Paper for Printed Library Materials.
ANSI Z39.48–1984. (alk. paper)

Library of Congress Cataloging-in-Publication Data

Foreman, Brian, 1972-
#Connect : reaching youth across the digital divide / by Brian Foreman.
pages cm
Includes bibliographical references.
ISBN 978-1-57312-693-9 (pbk. : alk. paper)
1. Church work with teenagers. 2. Church work with youth.
3. Communication--Religious aspects--Christianity. 4. Social media.
5. Online social networks--Religious aspects--Christianity. I. Title.
BV4447.F663 2013
259'.23--dc23

2013035119

#Connect

*Reaching Youth Across
the Digital Divide*

Brian Foreman

Also by Brian Foreman

How to Be #SocialMediaParents

Help! I Teach Youth Sunday School
(with Bo Prosser and David Woody)

For my wife, Denise, and children, Brock and Adria,

who let me play with shiny gadgets,

post pictures and comments about them,

and rarely get mad at me for it.

Acknowledgments

This book grew out of a conversation with my friends Victoria Atkinson White, Beth Kennett, Carla Smith, and Jeff Tippett. Little did I know that those chats would turn from brainstorms to gentle nudges and more. I'd also like to thank the people with whom I interact regularly on social media and in real life. They allow me to retell their stories and share in their struggles, and they teach me something new daily.

I must also acknowledge the parents and teens with whom I've worked and who inspire my passion for helping parents and teens communicate more effectively.

Contents

Introduction

Mason Wallace Park was across a road that became busier as the years of my childhood passed. The worst of it did not arrive until after those key years when my friends and I spent countless hours riding our bikes on the trails, chasing balls on the outfield grass, and cooling off in the concrete wading pool. We almost always had our parents' permission to go there. When we were children, a parent was always with us. As tweens, we checked in before going there. And when we became teens, before we had driver's licenses, we simply went to the park. By then it was okay for us to be there on our own—without our parents.

I remember a few things about that park. The first was how many people we met there from other neighborhoods, some who went to school with us and some who didn't. We were never at a loss for finding new friends, whether for the day or for years to come. We rarely felt at risk at Mason Wallace Park. When we did feel that something wasn't right, we either found a parent or crossed the road to our horseshoe-shaped neighborhood.

The second thing I vividly remember is the playground. The swings were monumental. You could swing out, looking down the hillside that ran to a creek a few hundred yards away. I have never been on swings that gave me the same feeling of freedom and flight. Then there was the wading pool. An eight-foot obelisk spouted water into the air and kept the foot-deep water circulating. It was never a neighborhood pool, but it was certainly a popular spot after impromptu games of softball and soccer in the heat of summer. There was also the park's gigantic metal slide. You flew down this slide, which was important because the sun heated it during the summer, and seared legs was the first sign of hot weather. Finally, the park had a merry-go-round. When we were young, parents spun us, taking turns to keep us entertained. Once adolescence arrived, the merry-go-round became a test of endurance and attrition. We challenged one another to endure the speed and not throw up, or to run 100 feet after getting off the whirling dervish.

No longer content to enjoy the gentle spin of the parent's pace, we sought adventure and speed.

I visited the playground at Mason Wallace recently. All the things from my childhood are gone, most replaced by far safer versions. The swings are entirely absent. A plastic playground now sits where the slide used to be. In place of the merry-go-round is a push-up station for a park-wide running and exercise trail. The concrete wading pool has become parking spaces. And something else is missing as well. While my daughter played on the playground, other parents watched one another warily. No one returned my efforts to talk. Many of the children played alongside one another as they might at an indoor fast-food playground—but not with one another the way we did when I was small. The only tweens and teens present were participating in carefully orchestrated league games, arriving in time to play and then leaving after a word from their coach reminding them of their next practice.

Today, our family lives next door to an elementary school with two playgrounds where there are no swings, no tall slides, no jungle gyms from which to hang upside down. During the day, the playgrounds provide boisterous sounds of children exploding from their classrooms. After school, some parents picking up their children gather to watch the kids play, all departing at some predetermined time. And the playgrounds are quiet. Children rarely just show up to play with the intention of meeting new friends.

Playgrounds have changed. The play equipment for my children creates a carefully regulated environment, by manufacturer, school system, and parents. And other new playgrounds have emerged. These new playgrounds are digital. Children, teens, and parents gather to play around screens. The new digital playgrounds are exciting and entertaining, interactive and connective. They are a part of our community fabric.

These new playgrounds give parents other reasons to worry, though. While conflicts of our youth were often forgotten the next day, on the new playground they are widely and immediately broadcast. When suspicious strangers showed up on my childhood playgrounds, we could easily identify them and were prepared to deal with the situation by departing or alerting someone else of their presence. On the new digital playground, strangers can take any identity that they want. On our old playgrounds, we learned how to socialize and relate to one another. The new digital playground does not offer that. Instead, we expect schools, churches, sports teams, and play dates to provide an arena where our children can learn social skills.

This book is intended to help you determine how you will engage with teenagers through social media, joining them on the playground because you know the risks are there. You know that we should not allow our teenagers to educate one another without adult experience and wisdom providing input and guidance. You also know that people of faith have a responsibility to be the presence of Christ to those with whom they interact. This should happen on the digital playground as well. For teenagers who are victims of poor behavior on this playground, aware and alert adults can provide healing and redemptive actions through real-life relationships.

Children are growing up in a world where the playground is digital. It is not new to them. It is normal. As usual, teenagers are early adopters of the new toys in the playground. Parents are left to play catch-up. As soon as we think we understand one new toy, another emerges. Try to imagine the way parents have felt in the past. In the 1950s, television replaced radio as a form of entertainment. TV was a new playground. Then came the rise of videogames in the 1980s, when Atari and Nintendo created a new playground. More recently, the Internet seemed like the ultimate playground.

Today, though, there is yet another new playground. That playground is social media. Just as I marveled at my parents' inability to program the VCR in 1986, I now marvel at my children who can negotiate the Internet through their Wii U. (Wii U and other gaming consoles—such as Xbox and PlayStation—are more than video game systems. They connect to the Internet, play DVDs, and even act as universal remotes for your home theater system.) Frequently I hear parents talk about teenagers and their cell phones or computers. They lament all the texting, tweeting, liking, and picture taking. If you listen to them, it seems that parents are left with limited options. We can ignore this new media. We can dismiss it as a fad. We can try to hide from it out of fear. We can embrace it.

I will take this a step further and suggest that we have two options. The first is to be present and aware of the new digital playground on which our teenagers are playing. The second is to use ignorance, dismissal, or fear as an excuse not to engage, leaving our teenagers to navigate the playground alone.

For many adults, understanding social media and the fascination it has for young people begins with reexamining teenagers. The first part of this book focuses on gaining a better understanding of Generation Z. While many in the church are still trying to grasp who the "millennials" are, Generation Z is rapidly coming of age. Both groups, the Millennials and Generation Z, and their distinctive traits will be examined. While each generation of teenagers has unique qualities and habits, youth also have a great deal of similarity from a human development perspective. The caution of defining teenagers through human developmental psychology is that our culture is redefining how long one can be a teenager—or at least act like one and be considered socially acceptable.

The second part of this book moves beyond who today's teens are and considers how teen identity is formed through community and social media. While churches ask questions about where young people are, Facebook and Twitter are already providing the answer. A discussion of how social media and community affect teenagers' sense of identity is important for parents and ministers. Teenagers are increasingly described as narcissistic because of the amount of media they generate. Have we stopped to consider that their content generation is a function and expression of their creativity rather than narcissism? How teenagers use social media to explore their identity is a key factor. This book also asks how teenagers define community. As churches emphasize the role of community, they must consider how they are helping teenagers create and participate in a new digital community. *Are teenagers being equipped to live faithfully in the digital playground?*

That question is central to the final part of this book. Moving from the "what" of social media to the "how" we engage is key. Do teenagers understand the image they project? Do they treat others not only kindly but also in a way that affirms their humanity? Safely behind a screen, it is easy to diminish others. The common behavior on forums, message boards, and even comment sections is often snarky and belittling. I follow college basketball, one team in particular, with probably an unhealthy level of interest. When I read the message boards for the team website, it is not uncommon to see people attack, belittle, or speak condescendingly toward one another. Keep in mind that these are usually people who are fans of the same team. A poster occasionally challenges this behavior. The response is never an apology but rather a "grow up, this is a message board," or "well, what did you expect." These are adults behaving poorly and abusively toward one another, and it is expected as part of the cultural norm. If teenagers did this, we would call it bullying. Why are we surprised if teenagers are bullies when they get behind the screen?

Teenagers need healthy examples of Christ-like behavior in every part of their lives. Youth ministries emphasize relationships. They encourage adult leaders to be mentors, to be present where teens are—at school, in the community, or during extracurricular activities. Most parents expect their children to have good manners when speaking to other adults. Churches teach using language of discipleship and witness. All of this is done with an emphasis on face-to-face interactions, but are we present with our teenagers on the digital playground? Are we mentoring them there? Are they seeing Christ-like examples? Are they using a language of affirmation rather than condescension? If we assert that the people of God should be the presence of Christ in the world, then we also need to recognize the digital playground as a part of that world.

Walter Brueggemann says that people of faith need to have a bilingual faith. He describes this in the context of the Assyrians' rule over the Jewish people (2 Kgs 18–19). In a treaty, the Assyrians demanded that the people speak the language of Assyria. Brueggemann called this the "on the wall" language. He described a second type of language, the "behind the wall" language. The Israelites used this language to remind themselves of who they were, how they learned, and how their history and culture shaped them. It gave them a way to remain authentic to who and whose they were, rather than being assimilated into the dominant Assyrian culture.[1]

Kenda Creasy Dean built on this idea with a third language, the "off the wall" language. Components of this language are symbols, art, and practices.[2] Social media is an "on the wall" language for teenagers today, but it provides an opportunity for teenagers to shape the experiences of the dominant culture using the tools of the "off the wall" language. It is not enough simply to educate teenagers in the "behind the wall" language and hope that they remain committed to their faith. We need to journey into the dominant culture with them and help them learn how to be the presence of Christ while they are there.

The playground is full, and more attractions and teenagers are joining it every day. One book cannot keep up with all the toys being added, and that is not this publication's focus. Rather, there is an opportunity and a need to be present with our teenagers on the digital playground, helping them understand their increased projection into the world through social media and how it affects them as young Christians called to be people of faith. This new playground challenges not only teenagers but also our understandings of community and our sense of self. My childhood playground never saw parents accompanying their teenagers at the frequency with which they did at a younger age. The digital playground is different. Adults need to be there, participating in the new means of communicating and building relationships, and teaching teenagers how to move the conversation from digital to analog.

Our teenagers are already on the playground. Are we going to be there with them? How can we choose not to be?

Make no mistake: the digital playground of social media has its own language. There are tweets, hashtags, likes, shares, pins, pheeds, and vines. The language is slowly making its way into our spoken vocabulary. Consider the first time you heard someone say "I need to process this," or "Let's take this conversation offline." The language of computers is already a part of our daily lives. Social media terms are entering our conversation as well.

A former youth, Matti, was telling me a story one day. After giving me the resolution of the story, she concluded with "hashtag, not thinking." Let's take a step back. A hashtag (#) is a symbol used in Twitter to denote a category for the tweet being posted. For instance, while watching the Grammys, you can follow a running Twitter conversation by searching #grammys. All tweets with that hashtag will show up in your timeline. Over time, the hashtag has also become a way to make a quick quip about the subject of the tweet. For instance, a picture is posted on Twitter of the user's dad in his 1980s MC Hammer pants. The poster might give it this hashtag: "#canttouchthis #dontwantto." In our conversation, Matti used a verbal hashtag to make a snarky editorial comment about the person in her story.

Ruth, a minister to college students, took this a step further. She has seen college students hold up two fingers, reminiscent of the peace sign, and swipe them vertically and then horizontally, thus drawing the hashtag symbol in the air. While making this gesture, they say the verbal hashtag. In Ruth's example, a young woman showed up for church after missing Sunday school. She saw Ruth and said, "I overslept and missed Sunday school." Then the young woman made the hashtag gesture and added in a deadpan vocal inflection, "sorry, not sorry."

The language is changing. Some individuals indicate that technology is changing and evolving too fast for most people to care. Those who work with teenagers or have teenagers in their homes do not have the luxury of not caring. There is no shortage of fears regarding social media and the digital playground, but perhaps the biggest concern is not being able to know what is going on in the lives of teens and young adults. This lack of knowledge is an intentional choice for those who dismiss social media and refuse to engage young people through it. Teenagers have a remarkable chance to influence those who are in contact with them on the digital playground. They also have the chance to be influenced. Who will teach them and walk alongside them, seeking to be the presence of Christ on the digital playground (#you)?

Before going further, I will define two key points that appear repeatedly. First, let's define *social media*, which involves three primary aspects. First, social media consists of web-based applications or portions of applications. It brought about Web 2.0, and at that point the Internet, which had been a way to gather data and information, also became a way to share and create information. The creating part is critical. It leads to the second aspect of social media, user-generated content. Social media applications give users the opportunity to create content through blogs (e.g., Tumblr), opinion sharing (e.g., Twitter), and multimedia (e.g., Instagram). These forms of creating content allow for additional sharing, discussing, and creating. The third aspect of social media is communication. By reading other people's content and engaging with it through feedback, we become part of a conversation, albeit limited and normally asynchronous. All three aspects define social media as a web-based and increasingly mobile form of communication that allows users to build connections by creating content and by interacting with others. It is changing the way individuals, organizations, and communities think, act, and communicate.

A second key concept that arises throughout the book is that of *presence*. There are two ways to be present with teenagers, whether as parent, adult friend, or minister. The first is to be actively connected and engaged with them on social media, whether through quietly watching what your teenager posts online and discussing it at home later or through an active interaction online in which you share and discuss openly with one another in the digital space. The second way is generally applied to parents who take a different role with teenagers by knowing their passwords or utilizing "social media check-ins" on a regular basis. The final chapter may help you decide which method is right for your family. Regardless how you do it, being present means you are actively aware of what is happening in the part of your teenager's life that is shared and expressed digitally.

Most important of all, and often overlooked, is that teenagers need to see positive examples of how to engage others through social media, whether those others are friends on Facebook or strangers in a comment section for the local newspaper. Teenagers see what adults post and how they interact with others. Being a model of good behavior and demonstrating Christ-like actions is one of the best ways you can teach young people in this new arena.

Chapter 1

Understanding Generation Z

Fifteen-year-old Scott is active in school sports and church youth group activities. He also enjoys a card game called Magic. This game is set in a fantasy setting where players build a deck of cards and compete with one another for supremacy. Though the game has been around for years, a new twist has recently occurred. Younger players started asking for ways to design their own cards. In computer language, we would call this "hacking." While the term "hacking" can mean breaking into computer systems and stealing information or creating havoc, it also denotes the ability to customize something. Burger King caught on to this idea early with its "Have It Your Way" ad campaign. Ice cream shops that custom-make your ice cream in front of you understand this idea as well. The Magic community created an online component that allows players to design their own cards (www.constructacard.com), print them, and share them with an online community that will offer feedback.

Fast-forward ten years into Scott's life, and imagine that the company for which he works has a top-down mentality. Scott is, of course, expected to follow the rules. But one day Scott thinks of a better way to do something. Upon bringing his idea to the company's attention, he is dismissed and told to do the task the way it has always been done. Scott is part of Generation Z. He is used to having the opportunity to make something better, and he views this directive as shortsighted and dumb. Scott may play by the company rules and do it their way. He is just as likely, however, to decide that he can do it better himself and become a competitor to that company. Some of us would judge Scott as rash and arrogant, but that classification is too simple. Scott is part of a generation of hackers, people used to customizing, seeking new and better ways to do something, and often not accepting of a "no" answer. To classify today's teenagers as millennials misses a key distinction in the differences between Generation Y and Generation Z.

Who is Generation Z? They are the digital natives, having never known a world without the Internet, at home on smartphones and iPads. Gen X gave way to Gen Y, a group of hopeful idealists experiencing remarkable change in society. They were the first group on Facebook. They lack the cynicism of Xers. And they are now giving way to Generation Z, the children of Gen Xers. Many people have yet to recognize the distinction between the two groups. First, Generation Z is a truly native population in the digital world. Born between 1990 and 2002, Gen Zers do not know a world where computers did not exist. Digital life is not an adoption for them; it is simply a part of their lives from birth. They lack the learning curve that many earlier generations had to face. A digital native is someone who has grown up in a world where the Internet has always been available at home. Whereas you may have been the family expert on programming the VCR, your children are quickly outpacing you in the digital world because their learning curve is so much easier.

Computers are enmeshed in their lives, and social media is such a large part of their experience that they do not know another existence. If you are a Gen Xer, try to imagine a world without television. Your parents had to forge through a new world of experiences, tools, resources, and fears that came with televisions and eventually cable television in the home. For Generation Y, the computer and Internet created new experiences, tools, resources, and fears. Now social media and mobile platforms are forming these things for Generation Z and their parents.

Second, Generation Y plays by old rules in the church and workplace, deferring to elders and senior colleagues. Generation Z, on the other hand, is a do-it-yourself generation spurred on by global access to information. Your political savvy may be better in some situations where opinions differ, but Gen Zers are more likely to say, "I can do it better, and I will." Incidentally, they just might. Technological advances and this mindset are changing education, moving it away from memorization and toward critical thinking skills and processing information. Generation Z may be the strongest society has ever seen at processing vast amounts of information, in part because they consume so much of it. The implications for this mindset extend far beyond the classroom to the future workplace, houses of faith, politics, and entrepreneurship.

Using these two broad generalizations about Generation Z (that they are digital natives with a do-it-yourself attitude), let's consider how digital culture is intertwined with them. Allow me to introduce you to a composite of the teenagers I have worked with over the last few years in my role as youth minister, youth minister consultant, or professor of Christian Education. Dave is sixteen years old. He does not call me on the telephone; he sends me texts. During group sessions I lead, if a question is asked or a fact is disputed, he can find the right answer on his smartphone via Google in seconds. Dave is proud of his vast music library and the personal playlists he created that blend music from across six decades. If he hears a new song he wants, he can download it instantly. Simply by keeping current with Facebook, Dave can tell you what people he has not spoken to in weeks are doing. Dave uses his phone for information, communication, photos, and broadcasting where he is, what he ate, and what he will do later.

Generation Z is connected. According to 2012 research from the Institute for Emerging Issues at North Carolina State University, 93 percent of teens from ages thirteen to eighteen go online on a regular basis. Broadband access is in the homes of 74 percent. From a hardware perspective, 70 percent own a laptop and 69 percent have an mp3 player. Combine this with Gen Z's do-it-yourself nature, and you will understand how they hack their way to personalized products. Seventy-eight percent of teens are accessing the Internet at school, up 47 percent from 2000.[3]

Social networking plays a large part in what teenagers are doing online, and they start young. According to the Social Media, Social Life study from Common Sense Media (2012), three-quarters (76 percent) of thirteen- to fourteen-year-olds have visited social media sites (and it's 87 percent for ages 15-17). Add to this the mobile component of social networking, and you understand why the percentages are so high. Here are other findings from the study:

- Two out of three (67 percent) teens have their own mobile device capable of connecting to the Internet, such as a smartphone, iPod Touch, iPad, or similar device.
- More than one in ten (12 percent) teens has "checked in" with their location from a mobile device, meaning that advertisers and others on the network will know where they are.
- Among teens who have a social networking site, half (52 percent) have checked their sites from a mobile device, and 43 percent do their social networking from a mobile device most of or half the time.
- The vast majority of teenagers have their own cell phones (82 percent), including 41 percent who say they have a smartphone, meaning they can use it to "check e-mail, download apps, or go online."[4]

During danah boyd's research about teenagers and their experiences with MySpace, eighteen-year-old Skylar told her mom, "If you're not on MySpace, you don't exist (2007)."[5] This statement may shock you for two reasons. First, you may be surprised that MySpace was once the preeminent social network. More important, though, Skylar's words make quite a statement about the digital age and teenage identity. This new generation interacts with the world differently. They define themselves differently. They socialize differently. They consume differently. They define community differently. Community is no longer a physical proximity or a singularly defined notion. What was once defined by residence, township, or house of worship now adds an extra category from the digital world. Technology has erased a number of physical obstacles so that people can connect in previously unimagined ways. Social media is designed for enhancing existing communities, helping others discover them, and building new ones. While Facebook provides a resource for connecting with and keeping up with friends, sites like Meetup and Google+ are conduits for meeting people with similar interests for the purpose of making new connections and finding places to grow one's interests. We will explore how this is dangerous for teens who are trying to redefine community according to such terms. Adults and our churches are struggling with this issue as well.

Developmentally Speaking

Raise your hand if you have heard this statement: "I don't understand that Twitter thing or why I care to see a picture of what someone ate for lunch." Raise your other hand if you were the one who said it. Now put your hands down, as everyone in Starbucks is looking at you. There is a misconception that sharing pictures, stories, anecdotes, links, and frustrations are habits of a narcissistic youth culture.

But your teenager is not a pathological narcissist. Your teenager is normal. Teens are often labeled as narcissistic because this stage of life is dominated by self-identity development. It is easy to make light of how much a teenager thinks the world revolves around her, but be honest: as children, we taught them as much. For babies, the world does revolve around them. As teenagers discover that the world does not in fact revolve around them (although I have meet a few adults who have not discovered this yet), they pour themselves into developing their self-identities. Part of this process is trying out who they are. Before social media, we did this on a different level. Our identities were labels that we wore—preps, jocks, Goths and so on. Many years ago, I had a teenage friend who ended the school year wearing black clothes, mascara, and black army boots. When I saw him mid-summer, he was wearing a bright pastel polo shirt and Rainbow flip-flops. I asked him what happened, and he casually responded that he decided to be someone different.

From a developmental perspective, teens are inclined to explore new things, share their thoughts, and engage with others. Are we giving them the tools to share their faith through these new avenues? If we accept that they are discussing sports, friends, family, school, and hundreds of other subjects via social media, are we providing developmentally appropriate means for them to discuss their faith as well? Consider the example of a church in Charlotte, North Carolina, where the youth minister encourages the congregation to tweet (using Twitter) during his Sunday opportunities to preach. Why does he do this? Will it not distract others during the service? His thought is that, if teenagers are allowed to participate in the sermon this way, then they are paying attention, sharing matters of importance to them, and sharing their faith with their connections. The feedback the minister receives by reading the tweets later is important. It allows him to see what subject matter resonates with people in the congregation, including his youth families. On a side note, it used to be considered an insult to a speaker when people where busy on their laptops, phones, or tablets while speaking. Now it is often the opposite. If I am with a group of teenagers and I say something that causes them to pull out their phones, chances are good that I will see it on Facebook or Twitter later, which is encouraging. While it is likely that I am in the minority, as I travel to conferences I consistently hear presenters discuss how much they like to search Twitter after a presentation to see what resonated with their audience. At a recent conference I attended, the speakers had a live Twitter stream on a screen behind them so all attendees could see what was being tweeted about the presentations.

Self-identity Development

Adolescence is a time of discovering the self and building one's identity. In today's teen culture, social media allows for new ways to do this. Creativity drives self-discovery. I feel certain that if today's adults had been able to access social media, we would have used it in similar ways. Thus, teens are not narcissistic producers of content. Rather, they are creative individuals with new forms of media through which to express self, explore self, and define self. As I wrote this chapter, two high school girls sat down at a table in Starbucks next to me and discussed their junior year schedules. One said to the other, "Smile with your drink. I'm going to Instagram you." There was no hesitation from her friend. If you think, however, that the old concerns of presenting your best self are not a problem for this group, who seem to share everything, then consider what happened next. The picture was taken and shown to the girl across the table. The subject of the picture responded, "That's awful! Take it again." After the fourth try, an approved picture was shared to Instagram, though it was presented as a quick and spontaneous shot in Starbucks.

Though the tools and media have changed, much about adolescent self-identity development has not changed. Human development theorist Erik Erickson described adolescence as stage 5 in human development, where the struggle is to attain ego (or self) identity while avoiding role confusion. Self-identity is about knowing who you are and where you belong in society. It involves compiling your experiences and your knowledge about the world and then shaping it into a strong sense of self. Abraham Maslow postulated that we seek self-actualization, which Carl Rogers called becoming a fully functioning individual.[6] Ultimately, all human development theorists suggest the importance of self-identity. Teenagers are exploring their identities with new opportunities, boundaries, and rules that are still being written.

danah boyd, who, among various other credentials, is a senior researcher at Microsoft Research and focuses on young people and social media, wrote,

> Today's social media have the potential to amplify age-old anxieties and rites of passage in ways that yesterday's communications media did not—by opening once-private exchanges for an entire school to see, adding photos and videos to words, allowing an entire community the chance to comment on what is seen or heard or said online, and by maintaining a permanent record of all those interactions."[7]

While the goals of identity development have not changed, the methods and tools certainly have. The rules and boundaries surrounding social media are evolving rapidly, and they apply in different ways as teenagers mature. As young people are given more freedom, their judgment process becomes critical. This happens as they mature, and parents need to be helpmates in the process. If you think all of this is happening at a rapid pace, consider experiencing it and navigating it while trying to determine your sense of self! For this reason alone, it is essential that parents are versed in the changing world and rules of social media.

How does social media affect how teens develop spiritually, specifically as members of the body of Christ? As parents and ministers, we must ask this critical question. Are we taking the time to reflect on how self-identity is shaped in the context of being a child of God? Do we compartmentalize this apart from the context of social media? The members of Christ's body are important in the various ways that they are living out the presence of Christ. Social media-savvy teenagers are a new part of the body, expressing new ways to be called and distracted. Part of the discussion around social media for teenagers includes how they are striving to be consistent on the new digital playground.

Let's pause to consider these questions. First, how does social media influence how teens develop spiritually as members of the body of Christ? The answer truly depends on the choices your teenagers make about to whom they are connected and the information they consume. For instance, if I only follow people who love the color blue, eventually I will either get sick of the color blue, embrace the color wholeheartedly, or start looking for others who are discussing the color blue in different ways. The connections that teenagers have will influence them. This does not mean they should only follow people who agree with your values and opinions. But, as they interact with different worldviews, are adults who care about them a part of the conversation? If a teenager in my group comments on a post, there may be an opportunity for a great conversation about the topic. For instance, I might ask, "What about that topic caught your attention?" Other questions might focus on the values in posts or where teenagers see God at work in a situation they are commenting on. We must give teenagers opportunities to discuss the things they see and read.

Will social media have an impact on their spiritual formation? It absolutely will, as will television, radio, and friends. The greatest difference is in the amount of information that is exchanged and how it can be used to persuade for good or ill, for the purpose of debating an idea or of harming another person. That is where adults can be guides who walk alongside teenagers through social media. When I was a kid, every parent in the neighborhood was a resource for my mother. If I were up to something mischievous, there was a good chance I would be seen and get in trouble. Conversely, I also knew there were plenty of adults I could talk to at my church when talking to my parents was difficult. I had positive relationships with adults as I went through childhood and adolescence. They were protectors, advocates, counselors, and advisors. I hope we are serving our teenagers in a similar way as we interact with them online.

Second, the idea of social media's impact on the spiritual formation of teenagers pales in comparison to how we take time to reflect on the identity teenagers develop as children of God. Do we compartmentalize their identity as children of God? At church, teenagers are placed in a youth group, apart from the congregation. They develop a spiritual identity that is separate from "big church." While the conversation of spiritual formation among our teenagers is interesting within the context of social media, it should be framed within a larger conversation of how this generation of teenagers has been taught a "nice" brand of Christianity, where good behavior is more defining of faith than the disruptive nature of the gospel as Jesus modeled it. Christian Smith, the principal investigator for the National Study of Youth and Religion (NSYR), describes teenage Christian spirituality as something that focuses on being nice and on the idea that good people go to heaven when they die. "Moral Therapeutic Deism," as he calls it, creates an individualistic form of spirituality that is generally disposed to a "whatever" answer when it comes to the gospel.[8] This notion that a teenager's spiritual formation occurs within a box outside of adult relationships, worship, and the confrontational nature of the gospel creates an individualistic, self-focused type of spirituality in which teenagers do not recognize faith as anything more than "playing nice."

Away from church, they learn to embrace their roles in extracurricular activities. They are developing as soccer players, class officers, or members of the band. Depending on the social environment, teenagers are able to cultivate parts of their identity that never influence the other parts. At age ten, my daughter received an e-mail from a friend who was upset with her for spending so much time playing soccer. The girl stopped short of offering my daughter an ultimatum of her friendship or soccer. When we are in relationship with one another, are we embracing all parts of the person or only those that fit what we need? Are we teaching our teenagers that their spiritual identity as a child of God is just one more item to compartmentalize, or are we teaching them how to be faithful people on the athletic field, in the band room, or during the school election campaign? These questions are far too broad for this book, but in consideration of social media, we need to teach students that what they say, show, and express online is a reflection of who they are and what they profess. To offer thanks to God in one post on Facebook and then follow it an hour later with a post riddled with slurs and vulgarity is problematic. How would a reader of the posts discern the real person who is expressing these things?

As adults working with, living among, and connected to teenagers, we should be willing to ask them the question, "How does this [post, comment, photo, etc.] reflect your beliefs?" We should be willing to challenge teenagers to think about who they are and, more important, whose they are. They are children of God during every minute of every day. This informs their identity in whatever activity they do. The adults in their lives have the opportunity to help teenagers avoid compartmentalizing their faith. Social media is merely one place where this occurs, but it is a place of growing importance for self-expression. The Bible provides us with examples of how God knows us. Here are a few:

- "For surely I know the plans I have for you," says the LORD, "plans for your welfare and not for harm, to give you a future with hope." (Jer 29:11)
- Jesus says, "I am the good shepherd. I know my own and my own know me." (John 10:14)
- "O LORD, you have searched me and known me. You know when I sit down and when I rise up. You discern my thoughts from far away . . . . Even before a word is on my tongue, O LORD, you know it completely." (Ps 139:1-2, 4)

The psalmist's words could be updated to say, "Even before a word springs from my fingertips, O Lord, you know it completely." For teenagers, the struggle of spiritual formation begins with the church's deeper struggle to teach the ways that being a child of God makes us different. Unfortunately, only 8 percent of teenagers from the NSYR study could talk about their faith as something deeper than how to be nice. Those teenagers were ones who pray regularly, attend worship services weekly, read Scriptures multiple times per month, and understand faith as an important part of everyday life.[9]

Again, while the topic of spiritual formation is far larger than the pages of this book, social media can play an important role for parents and ministers. By employing it as a tool for sharing Scripture with teenagers, asking questions about faithful responses to global situations, or even reminding them of prayer requests, social media can be useful for asking teenagers to engage their faith as a way of life rather than a mere part of it. There are Twitter accounts that send daily Scripture tweets (@Daily_Bible), blogs that provide daily devotions (www.d365.org), and youth Facebook groups where members share prayer concerns. We need to place these tools in the hands of teenagers, rather than hoping they stumble upon them. These reminders engage teenagers in their faith and connect them to others who are on the same journey. Youth ministers can also use social media to ask teenagers what they think about current events, reminding them to consider these events in light of what the Bible teaches. The efforts we make as adults to create faithful discussions with our teenagers is critical to helping them develop a faith identity that is not simply a compartmentalized facet of who they are, but rather an integral part of being a child of God. As they engage in these conversations and interactions, so do their friends and followers. While social media can be a huge distraction, then, it can also be a huge tool for sharing Christ's love simply through conversation.

Impression Management

In 1959, Erving Goffman penned these words in his book, *The Presentation of Self in Everyday Life*: "The true or real attitudes, beliefs and emotions of the individual can be ascertained only indirectly, through his avowals or through what appears to be involuntary expressive behavior."[10] Perhaps this was true in 1959, but in today's digital age, where opinions are shared through social media, you can get a good idea about the true attitudes, beliefs, and emotions of individuals. By being friends on Facebook or following on Twitter, I can learn a lot about the values and opinions of someone before a significant face-to-face social interaction takes place. Without the filter of immediate verbal and nonverbal responses, people often say things that they would not voice otherwise. The computer screen can act like the glass windows of a car. We have all seen someone picking their nose while driving, oblivious to the fact that we are watching them. The glass does not have magical properties. So just as our nose-picking, automobile neighbor goes without awareness, people sit behind their computer screens and say things that they might never speak aloud in another person's presence. This is not necessarily a bad thing; it is simply the truth. Frankly, I often find it refreshingly honest to know what a person really thinks about politics, religion, their brother-in-law, and sports teams. When we type, we are not nearly as worried about offending others.

Times have changed from when Goffman first wrote these words, but the concept of impression management and self-identity has not changed nearly as much as the tools of expression have. In his book, Goffman provides a framework for how humans behave in social settings and how they appear to others. The human condition leads us to care about the way we appear to others, both good and bad. Goffman presents three conclusions that are relevant to the discussion of teenagers and social media presentation. The first is familiar to anyone who has read the Golden Rule, which appears in nearly every one of the world's religions. Christians find this ethic of reciprocity in Matthew 7:12, in which Jesus says to should treat others in the manner we wish to be treated. *People should act toward others in the present in a way that would lead a just individual to treat them fairly in the future.* This idea seems logical, but things are not always so logical with teenagers. Teens are seeking their place in the world as individuals away from their parents, in new social systems of middle and high school. This leads to missteps, which are both natural and, though it's not always easy for young people to realize in the moment, not signals that the world is ending. By reminding them to present themselves in ways that lead to being treated as they wish to be treated, we show that the impression they give matters.

Disney has figured out this storyline. In the *Camp Rock* movies, Tess wants to be the star, and she treats people poorly, especially those she views as a threat. Mitchie, the protagonist is at Camp Rock not as a child of privilege but because her mother is the cook. Mitchie wants to be seen as one of the crowd and hides her family connection. Both characters have terrible missteps. Mitchie is outed by Tess and has to rebuild trust with those to whom she has lied. Tess, on the other hand, fails at the end-of-summer show because her mother, whose approval she desperately seeks, chooses to take a business call instead of watching Tess's performance. After Mitchie's redemptive moment, Tess fades into the background, only to be accepted by others later as a humble teenager. Both girls created false impressions. Both failed and were treated poorly as a result. Only when they revealed their true selves were they treated in the way that they craved all along.

The second conclusion is that *desired impressions can be reached through both acceptable and manipulative means.* Social media allows teenagers to put on different faces—in essence, to manipulate a self-impression. For some, this exploration is necessary and leads to healthy ends. Others get too caught up in what the proverbial crowd thinks. Many teenagers find social media a place to be authentic and real, perhaps their only outlet for that. They may reach the desired impression they want, or they may take the route that another person's opinion does not really matter if the person can't accept them for who they are. In *Traveling Mercies,* author Anne Lamott tells her story of coming to a conclusion that what others think about her is really none of her business.[11] This is refreshing on one hand, but it's hard to live by on the other. Many of us want people to think well of us, and when they do not, we have the choice to strive to fix it or to accept it. I think Lamott's realization as an adult has a lesson we could teach both our teenagers and ourselves.

Goffman's final conclusion is that *if we choose to live as performers, concerned with maintaining false impressions, we must accept the consequences of such a lifestyle.* Teenagers face this choice regularly in their exploration of self-identity. As a result, their social identity is partially defined by themselves and partially defined by others. Impression management is a key factor to developing a social identity. Teenagers must determine where they want to be situated within the social world they see, and parents can help guide them to a healthy perspective.

The challenge for the Christian teenager or family is twofold. First, how do we value and promote spiritual formation and development within the context of the Christian community? Second, how do we embrace the person God calls us to be? When we add the natural inclination to present an image of how we want to be perceived (rather than as we truly are), it can be difficult to answer these questions. It is especially difficult when we define the community as something other than the people with whom we have face-to-face relationships—that is, when the community is digital.

Youth are still becoming who God wants them to be. The good thing is that they are a little more aware of their self-identify with each passing year. Casting aside who they want to be, or who their parents or friends want them to be, and considering the person God wants them to be can ground them and put their spirits at peace about whose they are. Romans 8:26-29 tells us four important things about how God knows each of us. Teens need to hear these things, both online and offline.

1. The Spirit knows our weaknesses, and when we lack words for prayer, our groans and sighs are understood.

2. God searches our hearts and knows our minds.

3. We are called to be the presence of Christ wherever we are.

4. God knew us before we ever existed.

Parents and youth ministers have the unique task of holding a young person's deepest identity until he or she is able to see it.[12] Teenagers belong to God. They are loved. They have gifts to make the world a richer place. They are a reason for celebration. In congregations, they should find people who reflect their beauty as children of God back to them, showing it to them until they start to believe it. A parent's hope is for teenagers to surround themselves with people who will continue in this role. A teenager's identity is found here. It is felt through those in the congregation who embrace them. It is heard through those who teach and pray for them. It is seen through those who live faithful lives in front of them. Teenagers are still growing into the identity as children of God that many have held and sought for them.

The faith community helps shape our Christian identity and reflect back the people we are becoming. At a baby's baptism or dedication, the congregation makes a pledge to support the family in the rearing of the child, but also to teach the child the ways of faith. That is a tremendous commitment by a community of people. It suggests that a congregation values the spiritual formation of its young people—from babies to teenagers.

Independence

Imagine this scenario: You are fifteen years old, mere months away from getting your driver's license and freedom previously unknown. Suddenly, your parents hand you a list of 201 automobile driver responsibilities. Many of these feel like they are restricting your freedom beyond what your license is intended to do. Particularly offensive is the rule about your little brother riding in the backseat and wearing a helmet cam while you take him to soccer three times a week for six months. Is it a bad idea for your parents to keep you safe? Of course not. Is this a bit excessive? Perhaps.

You can implement many rules and products concerning social media that will be a lot like the helmet cam. You can track your teenagers' phones with GPS so you know where they are going. You can install apps that share their browser history with you. You can have strict guidelines about their privacy settings. You can sneak peeks at their computers and phones while they shower. Are these ways to keep your teenager safe? Of course. Are these a bit excessive? Grab your helmet cam. As Heather Horst wrote,

> In all these settings, youth may desire autonomy and independence from the rules and regulations of their everyday home and family life. However, given parents' concerns about and sense of responsibility over their children's lives and activities, most parents do not grant their sons and daughters full autonomy and control over their media and communications. Rather, young people's attempts to maintain privacy and ownership over their media usage and the media spaces where their engagement with new media takes place remain an ongoing struggle in their everyday lives.[13]

The negotiations over social media, digital communications, and privacy are national debates. They will likely be topics of debate in your family as well. Will your debate rival the effectiveness of national politics, will your home look like a police state, or will it be built on respect and trust? If you want to keep lines of communication healthy and present with your teenager, I would encourage the latter of the three. Developmentally, teenagers should seek their independence. If they're not given a healthy environment in which to do this, the results can be difficult to manage, if not disastrous for a period of the family's life. In the final chapter, we will discuss a few starting points for how to establish a respectful and trustful relationship with your teenager.

Growing up, I had a friend who was a talented volleyball player, likely headed for a college scholarship. At sixteen, she started dating an older guy who did not have her parents' approval. Within a few weeks, they forbade the relationship and placed numerous restrictions on her. This was before cell phones and the Internet, yet my friend still communicated with the boy and was driven toward him. Eventually, her resentment toward her parents grew too strong—a resentment they helped create, albeit out of love. In pursuit of this unhealthy relationship, my friend gave up volleyball, school, and her parents to be with the young man. Fortunately, the ending to this story is positive. They have been happily married in the years since and reconciled with her parents.

Teenagers do well with boundaries. In fact, boundaries give them something to push against. In a healthy relationship, there is great opportunity for guidance, teaching, and nurturing through this process. I have yet to meet a teenager who does not push against his or her boundaries. Some have done so with positive results and some less so. In the digital and social media world, parents have new boundaries to set, explore, and negotiate with their teens. Remember that teenagers are using this playground to explore identity and strive for independence. We want teenagers to gain a healthy independence; otherwise, they may end up living with us forever. (Shudder at the thought!) In later chapters, I provide a starting point and best practices for living in this new world together.

There is no particular point at which teenagers examine and challenge the faith perspectives of their parents. Some will reject everything and start building anew, while others embrace the faith of their parents. These are the two extremes of how the quest for independence may occur in teenagers' spiritual identity. For most teenagers, these extremes provide the boundaries within which they will make their own decisions. Parents who are have encouraged questions and conversations about the Christian faith will likely be more influential for their teenagers.

Keep in mind that there is no way to define self and independence without a discussion of context. We develop through our relationships and experiences; therefore, any discussion of the best practices for a family regarding rules, media, identity, and independence must begin with the acknowledgment that context matters. There is no stereotypical fifteen-year-old boy or seventeen-year-old girl. Certainly young people have similar characteristics, but they come from different families, circles of friends, and experiences. Parental perspectives and decisions are shaped by context and what parents have experienced. To be honest, part of parental concern comes from how we remember behaving when we were teenagers. Often, the parents who are most strict about a particular rule were either prolific breakers of that rule or had a sibling who was.

Oh, the stories we could tell our kids . . . but let's wait until they are adults!

Chapter 2

Implications for the Church

Social media has huge implications for church governance and structure. Generation Z may be more likely to resist the older ways of doing church. Those who continue to attend worship will challenge the status quo, while those who leave will become what David Kinnaman calls "nomads, prodigals and exiles,"[14] seeking spiritual answers but not in church settings. Nomads consider themselves Christian but view involvement in a Christian community as optional. They may also experiment with religion and spirituality as a whole. Prodigals are finished being involved in Christian community— and sometimes they are done with spiritual interests altogether. Finally, exiles remain committed to their faith but not to the institution where they learned about it. They see that God is active in the community and world around them but worry that the engagement of the Christian community is shallow and irrelevant. These young adult groups know that they have options, and they know how to be self-directed, critical, thinking learners. A collective force in this group begs for the church and the gospel to be life changing and relevant. The problem is that their voices are not heard. We miss them only when we look around and wonder where the young people have gone. Is the church capable of engaging the next generation? I believe it is, but we have work to do.

The church is challenged to ask the right questions that engage Generation Z. Unfortunately, the church often answers questions that this generation is not asking. As an example, in 2012 the North Carolina Legislature tightened laws banning same-sex marriage in the state. During the debate, the House Speaker said that while he supports the amendment, he predicts that it will be overturned in the next twenty years. Regardless of your view on this matter, it is wise to pay attention to the Speaker's statement, as it clearly demonstrates that the generations have widely different stances on social issues. I suspect that the conversations in our churches would yield a similar divide. More important, one generation promotes their stance with a biblical view of sexuality, while the other wonders what's the big deal. To one generation, the future of the family is at stake. To another, the issue is equality. The answers for the former group do not apply to the questions the latter group is asking. Those who teach Generation Z cannot rely on a model that dispenses authority. Instead, they need to engage in conversation. Giving teenagers a voice is critical to a discussion. Social media is a powerful way to do that.

While it is easy to indict the faith community as a whole for not asking the right questions, it is far more difficult to pinpoint the right questions for engaging this generation of teenagers. These questions fall into three categories.

Questions that are not a litmus test of dos and don'ts. Expectations that youth ministry can effectively modify teenagers' behavior have long hampered ministers. At one time, Bible studies that picked apart the Scripture concerning topics of sexuality, drinking, rock music, friends, and smoking were big sellers in Christian bookstores. They taught morals to teenagers and justified them with Scripture. But were the lessons helping teens create an incarnational faith, or were they simply aimed at creating moral young people who stayed out of trouble? We prayed for the teenagers who demonstrated risky behaviors and looked different from the others. As long as kids looked and acted the expected part, we youth ministers felt good about the job we were doing. More importantly, so did parents. This approach created a culture of moralistic teenagers for whom faith could be boiled down to a list of good and bad behavior. Teenagers today see and express life too transparently for that method to remain acceptable. Television shows and movies have heroes with major flaws. Sometimes the bad guys have qualities we celebrate. Oddly enough, the Bible is filled with heroes of faith who had major flaws. Moses argued with God. Abraham had an extra baby. Jacob lied to get the birthright. Saul killed Christians. Thomas doubted. Teenagers no longer (and to be honest, they never did) see the world in black and white. Boiling down the Christian faith to a code of behavior is not effective, so what is effective?

Behavioral litmus test questions set up judgmental attitudes and pull the community apart. Appropriate questions, on the other hand, bring Christians together into discussions where they are safe to challenge one another and it is acceptable to disagree. Rather than asking questions that apply contemporary culture to the Bible, ask what the Bible teaches about the human condition on issues of power, grace, forgiveness, resurrection, advocacy for the oppressed, and others. How do these teachings apply across time and culture? How does Jesus challenge the authorities, and what does that mean for us today? How does Jesus engage the outcasts in society and speak love into their lives? How does Jesus show awareness of the broken around him as he heals them? What does Jesus mean when he tells us to go and do likewise? When we ask teenagers questions like these, we open a different level of discussion that calls us all to a more genuine faith: a faith in which using others for personal gain or pleasure is unacceptable; where building others up is treasured over tearing someone down; where morals and right behavior are good, but merciful, redemptive actions are better. Teenagers know the right answers to questions in the church. Unfortunately, that may mean the questions are too easy. Trust that teenagers can engage with deeper, more timeless questions of the faith.

Questions that engage their faith beyond cognitive understanding. Deeper questions challenge a passive understanding of faith. They encourage teenagers to look for God in their communities and decide how they can make a difference as followers of Christ. Generation Z is acquiring its voice through multimedia, social media, and activism. Gen Zers can be described as a participatory group. They expect to be involved and heard. So when they are quieted or ignored, they will find a new place to share their voice. Christian Smith and Melinda Lundquist Denton say that the greatest threat to the spirituality of teenagers is their "benign whateverism."[15] The church should not worry about rebellion and risqué behavior. Instead, it should worry about the way Generation Z responds to faith with a flippant "whatever." Apathy is far more threatening to one's spiritual growth than doubt or skepticism. At least doubters and skeptics are engaging in the discussion. The "whatever" crowd could not care less because they have already deemed the discussion to be irrelevant.

I have a friend who is a passionate "foodie." We recently had dinner at a new restaurant that came widely recommended. About halfway through our entrees, the discussion turned to our food. When my friend asked what I thought, I responded, "It's okay." The horror on his face was tastier than the food. He told me that the worst thing I can say about food is that it is "okay." Apparently, my tepid response was more offensive to him than if I had said the food was terrible. If I thought the food was terrible, at least I would have to explain why. Do the flavors not mix well? Is one ingredient too strong? Was it served at the wrong temperature? You get the idea. But my response was a "benign whatever." The food was not interesting enough for me to have much of an opinion about it, good or bad. It was just okay.

If we interact with a generation of church-raised teenagers who have the attitude that Christian faith is just okay, then we need to rethink our approach. Perhaps the most critical question to ask is not about their response but about our culpability in presenting the gospel as something that earns a "whatever" response. That brings the conversation back to a generation that is passionate about media, their opinions, and the things in which they opt to participate. Use social media to ask questions about what teenagers are experiencing in their lives through world or community events. Encourage them to respond with a hashtag on Twitter or a comment on Facebook. Post pictures on Instagram, and ask if they see God in the picture. If so, where? The following questions/activities can help spark conversation:

• Where is God in this?
• How does this conflict with or agree with my faith?
• Why does my faith matter?
• How do I reconcile God's goodness in this tragedy I see?
• How can I minister and show compassion in this moment?
• Post a picture that you think shows the condition of your soul.

Questions that allow teenagers to tell their stories and adults to hear those stories. Do we really know what is going on in the lives of our teenagers? A pastor spoke to his youth minister after a Sunday service where two youth had shared their testimonies. He told the youth minister that he had no idea that teenagers were already facing adult problems. If the pastor of the church does not know what problems, issues, or crises teenagers face each day, then how can the pastor present a relevant gospel to them? Questions that encourage storytelling are essential. Relationships are key. They involve the telling and hearing of stories. Social media allows teens to tell snippets of stories. As adults, we should use those snippets to ask deeper questions about our teenagers' stories. While asking good questions is important, hearing young people's stories is even more important.

You see that a teenager has changed her status from "In a relationship" to "It's complicated" or "Single." Do you think a story exists there? A teenager posts on Foursquare (a social networking site that uses mobile phones to pinpoint locations) that they are with friends at a concert. A story is there too. A disturbing picture gets posted to Instagram. Behind it may lie a story in desperate need of being heard.

Equally important is how adults respond to teens' stories. Stories about a heartbreak or problem are not necessarily pleas for adults to fix the situation or offer sage advice. If we rush to talk, are we listening? Sometimes the teen simply wants to be heard and considered loved and significant. That means we listen, or we share parts of our stories. For teens, knowing that someone else has been there and lived through it is usually a great tonic to pain.

Ask questions that explore what you see in the social media stories. Ask questions that encourage stories. Use language that requires more than a "yes or no" answer. Starting questions with "tell me more about," "why," and "how" are usually enough for a teenager who wants to talk about herself. And most teenagers are usually glad to do that. We must engage with Generation Z using the tools in which they are already invested. They provide us with new avenues for dialogue.

As we return to the playground, keep in mind that social media can serve three purposes for parents and youth ministers. *First, social media can be a tool of engagement.* As mentioned previously, you can use what is posted online as a discussion starter or a story prompt. Social media can also serve the purpose of asking teenagers for input or opinions on ideas, topics, articles, photos, or videos. Creative ways of engaging teenagers on social media can enhance later face-to-face communication.

Second, social media can be used as a research tool. While you might research your teens' opinions, you can also be aware of important topics in the community or larger culture. For example, the "Trending" feature on Twitter alerts you to news, gossip, or important events in your community. It can also alert you to new memes, trends, and fads that are here today and gone tomorrow. Ask yourself how long the Gangnam YouTube parodies were going around before you were even aware of Psy. (And if that sentence made no sense to you, get online and do some research!) Additionally, social media can be a research tool for a topic you want to discuss with your teenagers. You can look for experts in that particular subject matter.

Finally, social media can help us stay connected and build relationships. Teenagers pay attention to the "Likes" on their Facebook posts and Instagram photos. They like to be retweeted or DM'ed on Twitter. A goofy Snapchat photo you send them will not raise your "cool" profile, but it will let them know that you are thinking of them. Simple actions through social media give you parts of the story, make teenagers feel affirmed, and tell them you care. While digital interactions certainly do not replace face-to-face communication, they do enhance it.

With these three tools in mind, let's return to the digital playground and see how youth ministers and volunteers might address some of the lessons and challenges teenagers face there. As we know, playground equipment evolves to be safer. With that in mind, let's assess the dangers and risks associated with the digital playground. We will also explore how ministers, volunteers, and parents can be cognizant of their teenagers' spiritual formation needs.

The Sandbox: A Spiritual Mixture, Part 1

The label "spiritual but not religious" is growing in America. Smith and Denton's research found that 54 percent of teenagers polled indicated that it is either "very" or "somewhat true" that they are "spiritual but not religious."[16] Generation Z is embracing this label as well. People who work with young people will tell you that this phrase is becoming increasingly more common, even among church kids. But what does it mean? The idea of a personal faith and a system of beliefs is growing and beginning to exclude the need for a worshiping community. Pair this trend with a lack of commitment to institutions, such as the church, and you can see why so many young adults and teens are using this language. It does not always mean they are abandoning the church; it simply means that they are more concerned with being identified as a person of faith than as a member of a particular religious brand. Many others are abandoning institutions altogether, of course, and are defining their spirituality through different avenues. These different avenues might look a lot like a sandbox.

Watch a group of small children play in a sandbox. They create and sometimes destroy. They might share, or they might hoard. They may play alongside one another but not actually together. As parents keep watch and talk, they may get the misconception that their children are playing together. In a similar way, as a member of Generation Z develops her faith identity, she may borrow from various faith traditions: a scoop of Christianity, a shovelful of Buddhism, and a bucket of social justice. Occasionally, a new scoop or bucket might be added, and the belief system is constantly evolving. Now take all of those who shape their faith this way and put them in coffee shops, on barstools, or in lunchrooms, and they discuss their thoughts with others who are doing the same thing. This amalgam of beliefs becomes a system where people are shaping and playing with their spirituality inside an unorthodox spiritual sandbox. It is where they share their beliefs and create new ones. It is where they hoard things they consider nonnegotiable but see other parts destroyed and rebuilt. By not being actively engaged in the sandbox with Generation Z, parents and churches are allowing young people to become spiritual but not religious.

A quick perusal of my Twitter feed from the last three hours reveals comments from people of different faiths about their respective religions. Two link to an article, while one refers to a spiritual observance. A similar exercise on Facebook reveals similar results. When I look through comments on two of the posts, I see people discussing faith issues from various viewpoints. Some who claim Christianity leave room for debate about what Christ they are following. When a teenager comes across these discussions or participates in them, we are wise to remember that they are still shaping their own faith and trying to determine what they believe. The sandbox gives plenty of opinions in addition to "facts" that are anything but factual. I would caution you not to jump into these conversations online in the attempt to bring your truth to the situation. Rather, be prepared to ask your teenager good questions about the issue (like those discussed earlier) in a different venue, perhaps face-to-face or through a private message.

Social media provides exposure to hundreds, maybe thousands, of different worldviews. Other people will ask good questions, except they are likely to challenge the litmus test of Christian belief, debate why faith in God matters, and embrace stories that provide community for people working out their beliefs. This is not to suggest that people are out there, waiting on teenagers to lure them away from the Christian faith. It is more likely that people are asking their own questions, and teenagers who are equipped merely to regurgitate Christian "dos and don'ts" may be targets for people who believe differently. When we are aware of those conversations and the fact that teens struggle with their own place in all of this, we are better equipped to assist in their spiritual formation. This practice involves using social media to be aware of what teenagers believe and of what they are exposed to. It means using social media to enhance further communication with your teenagers in the near future.

One effective idea is to post comments, thoughts, and links to articles, images, or videos onto your Facebook wall and ask teenagers to discuss them. This will give you an idea of where your teenagers are in their spiritual journeys. It also becomes something for you to reflect on and teach about later. Another tool is to use Instagram or Pinterest to post photos of things that challenge you, and ask your teenagers to consider what their faith says about those things. Encourage them to expand the conversation to others in their sandbox. These honest and welcomed conversations provide you with an opportunity to influence your teenagers to be more than "spiritual but not religious." It may even help them become disciples.

The Slide: A Slippery Place

The higher the slide, the better. Unless, of course, it's a metal slide and you use it in the heat of summer. Then you risk getting burns down the backs of your legs. As kids, we tried everything we could to make slides faster and consequently more dangerous. Our tactics included but were not limited to water, oil, cafeteria trays, and paper bags. The rush down the slide was great. On occasion, the dismount was disastrous. Regardless of the danger, we wanted the slide to be as slippery as possible. The culture surrounding Generation Z can be a pretty slippery place as well. Marketing has moved beyond simply selling to teens with a disposable income. Now many marketers sell the adolescent lifestyle to adults, and teens are along for the ride, which gets faster and more blurred between adolescence and adulthood. Consider video games and fashion as two examples. Video games are not just for kids anymore. You can find websites for adult gamers to meet and play so they do not have to be humbled by thirteen-year-olds with snarky attitudes. As for fashion, sit at a mall on a Saturday afternoon and count the adults who are dressed in clothes that only teenagers used to wear. My wife is so hyperaware of this that she takes me clothes shopping with her so I can ensure she is not buying things that will embarrass our teenager.

Generation Z receives multiple messages about growing up and, conversely, staying a child. Teenagers want to change the world but still battle a raging consumerism that is marketed to them every day. In their culture, being on the slide means seeing if things can be made bigger, better, and faster. The problem is that they lack the wisdom from experience that can prevent painful results. When adults avoid going down the slide with Generation Z, teens are more exposed to potentially dangerous messages and ethics. They are left to make decisions without the wisdom of a guide. They stand at the top of the slide trying to determine if ethics are relative, if being nice is good enough, and if they can in fact change the world and have everything that is presented as attainable. The anticipation of the slide is often better than the result.

The teenager who stands at the top of the slide alone, or who is encouraged only by his peers, may take a risk that a cautious, caring adult could deter with a simple question: "What makes this a good idea?" Today's culture makes the relationships between adults and teenagers even more important. Social media, the Internet in general, and the 500 stations on television are filled with a constant barrage of marketing images and ideas, concepts that further blur the lines between childhood, adolescence, and adulthood.

Marketers and messengers create subtler and savvier attempts to reach consumers. Take the fashion company OMG (www.heartOMG.com). On the company "About" page, you read, "At Heart OMG, we believe in sharing our faith & love through fashion while embracing our fun & characteristic lifestyle as well as giving back to the ones in need." The company also claims to be "Heavenly inspired and wonderfully made in the USA." While this may seem innocent enough, perhaps even something you could support, go the company's website and look at images of young women in suggestive poses wearing clothing with phrases like "Sweet Jesus," or read copy that says "More Jesus, More Fun," followed by pictures of the girls in bed together. To be clear, this is marketing genius. It is also hard to imagine that this company is truly what they claim to be. This is part of the problem with the mixed messages and slippery slopes of ethics that teenagers have to face.

Adults working with teenagers must be aware of the cultural messages that exist. My intent is not to be an alarmist but to suggest that a little knowledge goes a long way in helping teenagers with their spiritual formation and identity development. Teenage girls are bombarded with body images that project perfection. The models at Heart OMG are no different. The gospel is different, though. Ministers, volunteers, and parents who pay attention have the opportunity to ask how the gospel challenges cultural notions. Social media awareness points to the images and ideas teenagers are exposed to. While overlap exists across all communities, the teenagers in your community experience some particular issues as well. Urban issues in Chicago are different from those faced by teenagers in south Georgia or the Pacific Northwest. We are wise to pay attention to localized trends. This requires adults to be involved with the communication gateway of social media. Today's teens face many issues that previous generations faced, but the issues have new packaging that provides greater accessibility. Christian adults have lived the cultural struggles that teenagers face today. They have the scars to prove it and the wisdom to be guides to a younger generation. Walking through life in relationship with teenagers sometimes requires adults to be guides, and at other times it requires them to be companions on the journey. What matters most is remaining curious about what teenagers are exposed to, thinking about, struggling with, and celebrating. Relationships are not meant to provide kids with a moral police. Instead, they are to give them a trusted person who cares enough to love them through the good, bad, and ugly times. Social media cannot build that relationship for you, but it can certainly help you see into the lives of the teenagers with whom you are in relationship.

The Merry-go-round: A Head-spinning Pace

Generation Z has access to more information than any previous generation . . . often at their fingertips. Because of their ability to consume and process so much information so quickly, they are projected to be the smartest yet. The life pace of the average Gen Zer is dizzying. Aside from school, students are encouraged to be involved in multiple extracurricular activities, especially if college is in their future. Thus students complete their school day and then travel to a club, a practice, or an event. They participate in student government, sports teams (recreational or school-sponsored), book clubs, church groups, after-school jobs, community service, and an array of other activities. Then there is homework, time with family, and time for friends. I live near a busy high school. Aside from the school being used all the time, it is also in close proximity to a Starbucks (within walking distance, in fact). I avoid going in after school lets out because it is full of high school students drinking coffee and/or high-sugar drinks to get pepped up for the afternoon. They rarely stay more than a few minutes, but those who do are usually meeting for study groups. For that first half-hour, the baristas behind the counter barely have time to exhale as they provide the drug necessary for students to complete their days.

This is not a healthy and sustainable lifestyle for adults (although I am guilty of taking part in it), but it is even worse for teenagers who are still developing physically, emotionally, and socially. The idea that their lives are so production-oriented and busy is viewed as acceptable. Where is the wisdom of the church that promotes a Sabbath? When adults and spiritual leaders are not honoring Sabbath, how can teenagers be expected to do so? Instead, we all rush to the next thing, forgetting to give thanks for the now and reflect on what has been. As if we're being spun on a merry-go-round, the colors and images blur together in an exhilarating display at first, only to give way to a weak-legged nausea later.

In Psalm 46, the psalmist describes God as refuge, strength, and help in the ever-present dangers he faces. Curiously, later in the chapter he attributes these words to God: "Be still and know that I am God" (v. 10). We often define danger as an external threat to our well-being. We seek to protect teenagers from such danger, whether bad choices, texting while driving, or negative influences. Have we stopped to consider that one critical danger is internal? Are we a danger to our teenagers and ourselves on the dizzying merry-go-round of data, activity, and over-commitment? Sadly, many congregations are just as culpable as families, schools, jobs, and clubs that demand so much from our teenagers. We ask for Sunday mornings, Sunday nights, Wednesday nights, schedule-packed retreats, team meetings, small groups, and weekly activities. Youth ministers and volunteers rush from their families to go to the next ball game, concert, or awards presentation at one of the six high schools in town. Sundays come, and hallway discussions are about upcoming events, deposits, and meeting logistics. Worshipers make to-do or grocery lists during the worship hour. Where is Sabbath? Where is the obedience to God's command that we "be still"?

Social media gives the false impression that we are connected, building community and strong relationships. The question is often, "How do we connect with our teenagers?" Perhaps the better question is not about connections but about communion. Are we providing life-changing communion—both at the table and in our relationships—when we are together, or are we making plans for more activity? It may be time for congregations to have more conversations about how to judge ministry effectiveness. Are the best ministers the busiest ones, rushing from one event or meeting to the next, or are the best ministers the ones who spend quality time with teenagers and the adults working with them, making sure that God's love is pulsing through the relationships that exist? Programs are great, and they are needed to facilitate the communion of Christ's followers. But just as we are wise not to mistake social media for true community, we are equally cautioned not to consider a full calendar as equivalent to the incarnational ministry of Jesus Christ.

The Swing: Always a Seat for the Lonely

British anthropologist Robin Dunbar developed a theory about human relationships. It suggests that a limit exists for the number of relationships a person can maintain. Dunbar argues that "there is a cognitive limit to the number of individuals with whom any one person can maintain stable relationships, that this limit is a direct function of relative neocortex size.[17] He goes on to say that social networks do not render his number antiquated but instead "made us realize people don't know what these wretched things called relationships are."[18] If we are struggling to understand relationships in real life, imagine what confusion the concept of digital relationships adds. To suggest that all of our Facebook friendships are truly personal relationships is a poor definition of relationships. Yet if teenagers view relationships in such a way, it would suggest that this most connected generation is also susceptible to being the loneliest. The swing set is another playground staple that puts a person in proximity to other individuals but is ultimately a singular exercise. We swing next to others who are moving at a different pace and a different height. They may even face a different direction. Some need a push, while others pump their legs easily.

And so the person on the swing is technically swinging with others but is alone in his seat. Generation Z is digitally connected and in communication with others in rapid new ways, but that is not the depth of relationships to which Dunbar refers. Sitting in isolation, connected only by a smartphone, is a solitary endeavor, giving a user the sensation that they are in relationship with another person. It is true that some level of relationship exists, but the screen-based interaction is not likely developing the depth found in relationships with those we touch, see, and experience life with.

Dunbar's theory about relationships is a part of the design of Path, an application that allows users to post comments, locations, status updates, photos, and much more, similar to many other platforms. The difference with Path is that the user is only allowed 150 friends. It requires users to be more selective, with the idea that the sharing is more personal and important because the connections are more exclusive. Remember that Dunbar believed that only a limited number of meaningful personal relationships could exist at once. Whether or not there is merit to his science is irrelevant. What is relevant is that humans were created with the desire to be in relationship. In Genesis 1–2, Eve is created because it is not good for Adam to be alone. What a great lesson for us to remember and to teach our teenagers. The relationship inside the screen still falls in the realm of a person being alone.

That digital interaction alone creates a false sense of community—and actually isolates—is a subject of debate that will take years to resolve. The science simply is not conclusive on what technology and media mean in the long run for human relationships and communication. In the here and now, though, are teenagers who are reaching out for connections that they think mean community. It is essential that we think theologically about teaching our teenagers to consume and use media, particularly social media, in relationship to other people. We need to explore the stories about relationships throughout the Bible and ask what made those stories valuable. We need to explore the texts that demonstrate how the community cared for one another. We need to read stories from church history and community history that retell how families survived together or how neighbors helped in a crisis.

These living stories of the saints not only address the need for real relationships but also give a glimpse of how the gospel is lived out each day.

It bears mentioning that another form of isolation has nothing to do with social media. It is the isolation of teenagers who are not active in a church's youth ministry. Thomas sits in worship with his parents. He comes to Sunday school but prefers to sit off to the side and not interact with other teenagers. He does or says very little. He never participates in Sunday night or Wednesday night activities. Countless students populate the rolls of the youth ministries in our churches. They do not ask for attention, so we assume that they are simply not interested, or, if do try to make an effort at getting to know them, it feels awkward. Despite his low level of participation, though, Thomas is still a part of the youth ministry at his church. Adults need tools to help them connect and communicate with teenagers like Thomas. This provides one of the more interesting opportunities regarding social media. It can give you access to a teenager who is shy or hesitant to engage in person. It might eventually provide him with the necessary level of comfort to engage with an adult face-to-face. Encourage a teenager like Thomas to be friends with you on Facebook, or let him know that you are going to follow him on Twitter. When you do this, look for posts that reveal a bit about who Thomas is, so that you might start a conversation with him the next Sunday you see him. With teenagers like Thomas, be clear that you would like to be connected to him on social media. This intention communicates two things. First, you are not a creepy stalker from his church. Second, you notice him, and getting to know him is important to you.

Emerging Identities

Paul (a youth culture consultant from Toronto) and I were talking about teenagers. He shared this line with me: "Today's youth and their media are inseparable." As danah boyd's earlier story about MySpace illustrates, teen identity has a social-media component that grows the more time they spend in the digital playground. A parent shared a story with me about a struggle in their home. Tom, his wife, and his fourteen-year-old daughter had a difficult discussion at dinner one night. Leaving the conversation with tension still high, Tom's daughter took to Facebook to express her frustrations. She shared more than her father was comfortable with, and when he discovered the post an hour later, a new fight ensued. This one involved what was okay to post. He wanted her to remove the post, and she refused. She had also changed her passwords so that he could not delete it himself. This was yet another point of conflict. Everyone went to bed angry. The next morning, the post was still on Facebook. After his daughter went to school, Tom hacked into his daughter's Facebook account and deleted it.

I was telling this story one time, and a slip of the tongue I made at the end gave me pause. I mistakenly said, "Tom hacked into his daughter's Facebook account and deleted her." At this point, some people applauded Tom's response, while others became uncomfortable with it. Aside from the fallout between parent and child on this issue, there is the real issue of the daughter feeling deleted. Her pictures, thoughts, and communications that were stored one day were gone the next. That part of her identity was deleted. A quick caution: Do not read this story and rationalize it as an adult. Instead, think about it from the perspective of that teenager. Her perception is her reality in the moment. Her father intentionally deleted her from Facebook.

In chapter 1, we discussed self-identity development. Much of that discussion was based on the development of the individual. We also need to examine the role of community. In the next chapter, we will look at the differences between connections and community, particularly as social media defines each one. Next, we will consider the role of social media in defining teen identity and community for teenagers. Finally, our focus will turn to how someone who is connected and social can also be void of true community.

Chapter 3

Community and Social Media

What Is Community?

It is likely safe to claim that neither Jesus nor Paul would have described community in the absence of other human beings. The world we inhabit does. It is important that we distinguish between the two understandings. When describing human communication and relationships according to social-media applications, I will use the word *connections* or some derivative of it. For *community*, however, I will use Peter Block's definition: "Community is a place—geographically bound—where people are physically connected and have an enormous incentive to pursue a common interest."[19]

There are many definitions of community, but Block's simplifies the idea into several characteristics. First, his definition calls us to recognize that the core of the community is a geographic place. I'm grateful that I can be connected to other people from around the world through digital media. This exposes me to new ideas, images, and cultures that I could never afford to visit in person. But just because digital connections are good does not make them a community. The things that affect daily lives happen in a geographic place. If it snows in my southern city, I have to rush to the grocery store for milk and bread. People in the Northeast think Southerners' reactions are crazy. We can talk about and understand the differences in those cultural norms, but cognitively understanding them is not the same as experiencing them in relationship or proximity to one another.

Second, Block's definition indicates that community requires people to be physically connected. The physical connections range from our roadways to our restaurants to our churches. They mean that we have access to the same people and experiences each day. This is, of course, more difficult in larger cities, but my neighborhood within the city is a community. I see my neighbors frequently at the grocery store, the YMCA, the shopping center around the corner, and restaurants within walking distance. We are physically connected. We have access to similar experiences each day. This creates the opportunity for conversation about issues, needs, and wants for the community.

A faith community is similar in that regard. The physical connection is the church building and, ideally, is fully realized in worship. Our connection to God and one another is the proverbial tie that binds. Although congregations may not be composed of people from a neighborhood around the church, the physical connectedness of Bible study, worship, fellowship, service events, and trips builds community.

Third, Block's definition asserts that those in a community have an "incentive to pursue a common interest." When an issue arises within a school system, the rallying cry is not heard across the country. When a neighborhood experiences a violent crime, the call is not heard in distant corners of the world. When a family is forced to choose between groceries and medication, a stranger on a different continent does not provide the assistance. The people in the physical proximity of a community respond to these common interests. Neighbors and parents gather to meet with the school board. Neighbors meet with police officials about their safety. Neighbors and church groups provide assistance to pay bills, distribute food, and see someone through a difficult time.

True community requires shared space and shared experiences. Faith communities gather with a common interest to worship God and learn to be the presence of Christ in the world/community around them. Relationships are built on this premise. People are served based on this common understanding. Adults, youth, and children learn in community, serve as community, and prepare to provide community to others.

To reiterate Block's definition, "Community is a place—geographically bound—where people are physically connected and have an enormous incentive to pursue a common interest." The enormous incentive for churches and parents is to live out Proverbs 22:6, "to train children in the way they should go, so that when they are old they will not depart from it." That is one of the common interests of the church and the parents within it. Social media is a tool for training children, but it will never replace the relationships of the community. We must admit that social media does have a place, but its place is still being defined.

In the world of social media, community is defined as the people who are participating in a particular discussion. For instance, corporations, nonprofits, and churches hire community managers for their social-media accounts. The goal for the manager is to build an online presence for the organization that acts to engage digital followers. For some, the ultimate goal is to sell a product or to raise awareness about issues. Other goals include developing brand loyalty, monitoring brand awareness, or getting community feedback on new ideas. The ultimate goal, however, is engaging people, facilitating conversations, sharing narratives, and creating opportunities for participation. NBC's program *The Voice* does this well by using Twitter. Each judge has tweets cued up for the shows. Their accounts are promoted, and the tweets are shown across the television screen at appropriate moments. Between episodes, the judges engage with their followers, which serves to promote the shows. Regular fans feel like they have access to famous personalities like Blake Shelton or Adam Levine. When those judges retweet or respond to fans, they build loyalty and become brand evangelists for *The Voice*. Generation Z is a participatory culture. This kind of access gives them the chance to participate.

Another example is Fox's program *American Idol*. After the initial elimination process by the show's judges, judging becomes the viewers' responsibility, and people are allowed to text and call in. Teenagers cue up to vote for their favorites. Regular weekly votes exceed 50 million, topping out in the 2012 finale with more than 132 million.[20] This is a generation of participation; teenagers enjoy adding their opinions, their unique twists, or their own story lines. While Nike allows customers to choose a shoe design, select their own color scheme, and add other touches (such as their names to the tongue of the shoe), institutions that fail to recognize this trend and adapt will be ignored by a large segment of the population.

Television is also changing beyond reality shows. With applications like Viggle, viewers use their phones to listen to the television show that is currently airing in order to identify the show and post their presence as watchers, talk about the show, get hints about upcoming story lines, and vote in various opinion polls. As this opportunity to connect with other users grows, teens get more and more connected to other people. They participate in digital communities run by digital managers. They see others' faces and even a few carefully chosen facts about them. Some other users are called friends. All of this can happen from the sofa while teens use a laptop, tablet, or smartphone. Users can be a part of a community, though literally no other living soul is within earshot.

Social media is more than Facebook, Twitter, and Instagram. It also includes texting, gaming, and exploring. It involves food reviews and movie check-ins. For ease of discussion, I will divide social media into multiple categories: (1) relationships and communication, (2) photos, (3) location, (4) music, (5) special interests, and (6) new ideas and design.

Social media is most often accessed through applications and platforms. These applications, or platforms, are not exactly one-stop shops for all the ways teenagers will communicate and express themselves. While Facebook may be the biggest entity, it does not do what several other platforms can do, or it does not do it as well. In the last year alone, Facebook has purchased a photo-sharing application, Instagram, because the latter does photo sharing far better than Facebook can, while Twitter has introduced its own version of photo sharing so that its users don't need Instagram. Twitter meets a need that is different from Pinterest (which is like an online bulletin board for posting links to ideas and interests), and Foursquare provides a service that Path does not. Teenagers are using many of these apps—and sometimes all of them!

As we explore the categories below, I will provide a list of applications that fit each category. These lists are not intended to be hard lines of distinction, nor are they comprehensive. See www.socialmediaparents.com for more in-depth information about the inner workings of the apps on these lists. This website regularly posts reviews about new apps as well.

From Hi-Tech to High Touch

The idea of being connected, having lots of friends and followers, is perfectly built for teenagers and the popularity culture. Think back to the end of one of your school years when yearbooks were distributed. Signing those books and having yours signed was a big deal. For some, the quantity of signatures was the primary motivation. For others, the quality was more important. Social media is the same in that regard. It affirms relationships and provides a means for communication. With so many applications through which to communicate, teenagers are in constant connection with data and stories. But often, they are not in connection with genuine, authentic relationships. Though it can facilitate interaction between true human engagements, social media should never be considered a relationship builder. It is our responsibility to help teens move from hi-tech to high touch.

When working with a group of ministers who work with teenagers, smartphones, iPads, and laptops are as prevalent and acceptable as cups of coffee. And these devices aren't just present during breaks. They are present during meals, seminars, workshops, and worship. They are seen in lobbies, elevators, sidewalks, restaurants, bars, assembly halls, and classrooms. Many are communicating with others at the conference or with friends who could not be there. Many communicate with family. Regardless, the tweets, Facebook posts, and text messages are a large part of the function. One cannot help being aware that these are people who know teenagers well and are early adopters of their communication tools. I started texting on a Nokia phone, IM'ing when AOL was still a player, and joined Facebook in its second year. That is where my teenagers/college students were.

A friend e-mailed a quote from a conversation he had several years ago: "Someone said to me, 'Young people and media have become one. We can no longer separate a young person from their technology.'" I agree. We have a hi-tech population of teenagers. They want communication. They consume media. They produce content like no other generation before them. Sherry Turkle titled her book *Alone Together*. The subtitle is "Why we expect more from technology and less from each other."[21] If teens and their media are inseparable, then parents and people working with teenagers must seek ways to reverse the trend Turkle describes.

As humans, we long for human interaction. We long for touch. From the earliest chapters of Genesis, we read that it is not good to be alone. We have to model for teens how to balance the hi-tech world with our high-touch needs. As adults, that means we have to learn how to do this as well. There should be no more dismissing, ignoring, or being fearful of social media and teens' use of it. In fact, those three excuses are lazy responses. Anyone can do that. Learning how to play in the digital playground with your teenager takes time, energy, and effort. It means communicating face-to-face about your presence online together. How do we do that? The following four points are from a blog series I wrote for parents to consider how we move from hi-tech to high touch.[22]

Connections versus Community

As we talk about community, connections, and social media's role in human relationships, it is worth noting that teenagers want communion, not connections. Social media and technology already allow us to be the most connected generation that has ever existed. There's no need to read cave drawings or wait for carrier pigeons. Instead, just check out Twitter and Instagram. Our ability to connect is instant and sometimes fraught with peril. Parents are concerned about whom their teens are connected to and what they might share. We could even argue that social media is causing our teens to become anti-social (which seems ironic). Others suggest that we need to use social media more in education to spark innovation and creativity. Incidentally, this is not only a teenage interest. I meet adults regularly who want to connect through the professional network, LinkedIn. On more than one occasion, they have said that more connections make them look more important.

I have several hundred "friends" on Facebook and connections on LinkedIn. You might have them too, but if we are honest, many of them are neither friends nor even people we keep in contact with. That does not make Facebook or LinkedIn bad. On the contrary, the connections are useful and helpful. It is almost as if rapport already exist because we are connected digitally. While technology offers us connections, however, getting high touch provides us with community.

Teenagers who use social media tend to have lots of connections, but they will also tell you that community is their preference. Community is a product of relationships, friendships, shared experiences, and common bonds. Community provides a group to laugh with and a group to cry alongside. Community inspires teenagers to be more than a screen name. Parents bear a role in this effort. We need to try to teach our children the role and value of community. We model it by participating in civic groups, faith groups, book studies, and poker night. We encourage it by allowing friends to come over and eat our food and play our games. We facilitate it by driving to and from soccer practices, youth groups, and band rehearsals.

We can use social media to make connections and broaden interests, but true relationships come from interactions that are cultivated and grown in real life, not through a device. I have made plenty of business and mutual-interest connections online that became real-life friendships. They may have started through social media, but the act of sitting down for coffee the first time is what transformed them from digital connections to human relationships.

Fears and Failures

Our family celebrates two great dates in April, a wedding anniversary and the birth of my daughter. Sadly, we often find our celebrations muted by tragedy or the remembrance of tragedy. The list of sad events in April is well documented. Just in the last two decades, our history books have been filled with unspeakable tragedies, some caused by humanity and some by acts of nature. The events do not need description; the names alone evokes images—Waco, Oklahoma City, Columbine, Virginia Tech, Alabama tornadoes, Boston Marathon. Each time such events occur, we adults are stricken with grief and horror. We make donations, offer prayers, and promise solidarity with our brothers and sisters across the land. I wonder, though, what impact do the tragedies have on our teenagers and children?

I shielded my children from the images of September 11 on the ten-year anniversary, perhaps protecting my own psyche as well. I do not even watch the show *Mad Men* because of the graphic of the man falling from the building. I am careful about what images my children see, but I can't hide them forever. Thinking through this as I reflected on the Boston bombings and the Newtown shooting victims, I was struck by a tweet I read hours after the bombing occurred. It was retweeted by a teenager I have worked with in the past as a minister, and the original came from her classmate. It read, "When did the future switch from being a promise to being a threat?" Youthful optimism has always been a hallmark of adolescence. Generation Z, however, is growing up with images of violence and terror. I hope we are paying attention to our teenagers. They need to be affirmed that from tragedy, where we see the worst of humanity, we also see the best in the helpers. On these occasions, nothing replaces face-to-face interaction with your child.

1. Have age-appropriate conversations with your teenagers when tragic events happen. Ask what they have heard, because misinformation is usually worse than the truth. Ask how they feel about it. Ask if they are scared.

2. Watch their body language and mood changes through the next few days and occasionally offer to talk.

3. Teach your teenagers about hope amid tragedy. Look for the helpers and heroes. Look to the survivors who go on to change their corner of the world.

4. Model resilience, compassion, and promises of the future.

5. Hug them and tell them you love them.

Screens and Screams

I eavesdrop . . . a lot. It is probably not a great habit, but I'm good at it. As you can imagine, hearing two mothers discuss their teenage sons' video-game habits and social-media use got my attention. The conversation centered on two complaints and one appreciation: the amount of time spent on the games, the distraction of hearing one-sided conversations during the games, and the appreciation that gaming kept their sons from bothering them.

The first two points made me smile and wince at the same time. The third point was painful to hear, but I'll address it later. According to an industry insider, more than 183 million people in the United States play video games regularly. Here are more of her statistics:

• The younger you are, the more likely you are to be a gamer—99% of boys under 18 and 94% of girls under 18 report playing videogames regularly.
• The average young person racks up 10,000 hours of gaming by the age of 21—or 24 hours less than they spend in a classroom for all of middle and high school if they have perfect attendances.
• 5 million gamers in the U.S., in fact, are spending more than 40 hours a week playing games—the equivalent of a full time job!
• Over 3 billion hours per year are spent playing video games by people on planet Earth[23]

It should come as no great surprise that teens spend a lot of time looking at screens. Some have balance in their lives; others do not. We, as parents, should pay attention to the collective amount of time our children spend with screens. Frankly, we should also do an honest assessment of the time we spend with screens.

If you have ever listened to one-sided conversations, it can be humorous. Listening to teenagers talk "smack" to one another playing video games is also usually humorous. To me, it is striking that the mothers were unaware of who was on the other end of their sons' conversations. These mothers laughed about the fact that their kids might be talking to friends, a college athlete, or some stranger halfway around the world. I think it is important that we know who interacts with our kids and that we teach our kids the tools for recognizing when it is time to disconnect from someone else.

This leads directly to the third point in these mothers' conversation. They let the boys play games as a means of keeping them occupied. As a parent, I am also guilty of allowing a book, screen, or art project to baby-sit my children from time to time. As I listened to the women talk, I was acutely aware of my own culpability in this area. I cannot judge whether someone allows technology as a temporary distraction or uses it as an abdication of parenting responsibilities. What I can say is that I had to reflect on this topic and how I replace screen time. I suggest replacing screens with family screams—that is, with fun times spent together. Here are a few I suggest:

- Go bowling and eat bowling alley food for dinner (if you are lucky, it will be good).
- Ride bikes on the greenway or through your neighborhood.
- Play board games together.
- Try new experiences like community theater or minor league baseball.
- Give gifts that create memories rather than clutter.

Have screams of delight together! Let your teenagers bother you, and create new memories that you will laugh about later. Great parenting is a decision that requires effort and planning.

From Significance to Insignificance

"You do not have many friends. That's okay. God does not want you to." I overheard these words one Saturday morning as a young adult counseled a teenage guy. It was tough to ignore. I have a problem with the statement that God does not want this young man to have friends. Teenagers already struggle with rejection from other teenagers, friends, and sometimes parents. I certainly do not want them to think God wants them to be lonely too. Is it healthy for teenagers to walk through their lives thinking that everything related to their social standing is determined by God? Popularity or social leprosy is not a predetermined character trait from God.

Insignificance is a tough feeling. People make others feel insignificant. We do this through thoughtless words or actions. We do this intentionally and by accident. Teens experience this online and through social media in a variety of ways. Here are just a few:

- Her picture doesn't get many likes on Instagram.
- People make mean-spirited comments on his Facebook page.
- Someone spreads rumors through Twitter.
- She sees Instagram photos of friends at a party she wasn't invited to; in fact, she was never even told about it.
- They have "Facebook envy" because everyone else's life seems so much better.

Teens may even reach out through social media for help, only to be ignored or rebuffed. What do we do about teenagers who feel insignificant? Do we give them clichéd answers that place the blame on God? Do we dismiss their feelings with "it will get better soon"? Do we try to cheer them up with smiley-faced emoticons or a clever e-card? None of these responses is acceptable.

When people feel insignificant, they need someone to walk beside them and hear their story without trying to fix it through empty words. When people feel insignificant, they need someone to be a genuine encourager, affirming their gifts and talents. When people feel insignificant, they need high touch that reminds them that they are alive and they mean something to another human being. When people feel insignificant, they need those who love them to hold them until they find their footing once again. Social media cannot do this, but Christian community certainly can . . . and does!

Consider these tips to help move a teenager back to feeling significant:

1. Listen to them. Turn off the TV and sit at the table to talk. Listen deeply and be slow to respond.
2. Do something your teenager enjoys doing (bowling, folding origami, playing a board game, tossing the ball, painting, shopping).
3. Hug your teenager.
4. Affirm the little things that might be easy to let go unnoticed.

Social Media Applications

To this point in the book, we have discussed social media in rather broad terms. There are, however, numerous types of social media, and they are integrated in ways that you might not have considered before. Here, I offer several applications for each category and then explain how they may be used.

Relationships and Communication

Facebook
Google+
Path
Twitter
Snapchat

While these apps have multiple functions, the most basic is communication. Facebook users can keep up with the lives of their friends, share their thoughts and opinions, and send messages back and forth. Google+ is focused on helping users build and expand networks around common interests. Path offers many of the same functions of other apps, but it allows users only a select number of friends. Twitter offers the opportunity for quick posts where users can share, browse, and communicate with one another in 140 characters or less. Snapchat is a photo-messaging app in which users send pictures with creative messages or doodles on them. (Note: While the pictures disappear shortly after the person views them, they are still accessible later.)

It is worth noting that writing letters is becoming a lost art. Letter writing facilitated interaction in a similar way to these apps, but with one critical difference. Letters were never instantaneous, quick-hitting thoughts. Letters involve carefully chosen words, sentence structure, and often an emotional investment in the story being told. Of course, this is a romanticized version of writing letters, but when a composition is intended for only one person, requiring thought and intentional effort, it is easy to romanticize handwritten letters. One of the values of letters was the ability for writer and reader to remain connected during physical absence. The anticipation of the post heightened the experience. E-mail lacks that kind of anticipation, but it does keep people connected one on one.

Photos

Instagram
Flickr
Picasa
SmugMug
Rando
Albumatic

Photo-sharing applications are likely to be integrated into larger information-sharing platforms. Instagram is one exception, as the pictures are the centerpiece of the application. Even so, Instagram pictures can be shared through multiple sources, like Facebook, Tumblr, Twitter, and Foursquare. Other applications like Twitter, Foursquare, Path, and Google+ include their own photo-sharing capabilities. The cross-application sharing is a convenient tool for users who do not mind everyone seeing the same material. Some people, however, may want their photos more protected than their tweets, so they choose not to share across all platforms. One of the remarkable qualities of social media is that it allows users to customize their experiences and interactions.

A picture is worth a thousand words. In some of these applications, users can add words to their pictures through comments and affirmations. While many positive comments are shared, it is worthwhile to remember that negative comments come through as well.

Other applications serve different purposes. Flickr, Picasa, and Smug-Mug allow users to store and share pictures and albums online. These photos can be indexed, categorized, searched, and even sold if the user wishes. A small twist on these is an application called Albumatic, which lets you choose albums that friends can contribute to. Google+ does this as well, but because this is Albumatic's only function, it is easier to use. Why would you use it? Imagine that a group of friends go on vacation together. By taking pictures through Albumatic, they can share their memories without bulky downloads and file transfers. Rando is lesser known but definitely an app to watch, as it allows users to upload photos that are randomly shared/exchanged with another user. This may seem odd to many, but if you are creative and want to see how strangers respond to your work, this is a great place to share and to draw inspiration.

As previously mentioned, some apps overlap, and photo-sharing functions are major components of relationship-based applications. Social media offers the flexibility of having opportunities to share in both larger capacities and more specific ones.

Location

Foursquare
Forecast
Localmind
Banjo
Glancee

Location-based applications provide the ability to share information about where you are or where you will be. Each app listed above has unique uses. Foursquare is the best known and most comprehensive. It also integrates with many of the relationship-based apps, allowing you to share your location or pictures from that place, event, or happening on Twitter and Facebook. Technically speaking, Foursquare is a location-based marketing system. More generally, it is a check-in app where users are able to announce where they are, who they are with, and what they are doing there. In the process, they earn points and badges of accomplishments. The incentive for check-ins is to compete with your friends for points or to earn badges of accomplishment. One especially unique incentive is the Mayorship feature, which often provides perks for the Mayor of a location, a position that is earned through the most check-ins at one location. Because Foursquare uses GPS locators in users' phones, it is mostly a mobile platform, but you are allowed to check in at a location prior to arriving, so some people use this feature on their laptop or desktop computers.

In Forecast, users share where they will be. People use this app to let others know their calendar, whether they are on time, and where they can connect with them later in the day or week. If safety and privacy are a concern, then Forecast may not be a good option for you or your teen, but ultimately this depends on whom you are connected with through Forecast and how much you feel comfortable sharing. A youth minister might find Forecast helpful for letting teens and parents know that he or she will attend a game or work in a coffee shop for a few hours. This allows followers to know where they can make an "unofficial" visit to the minister to talk or catch up.

Speaking of privacy and security, it is important to understand how the remaining three apps on the location list relate to other check-in applications. All three use information the user shares on other platforms, like Foursquare or Google Checkin, to aggregate information about other locations. Here's an example: I am planning a trip to the mall. There is a big sale at the Lego store. I open Localmind to see if anyone has checked in there, and then I post a question about how crowded it is or the best place to park. Users who are on Localmind will be notified of the query and can respond. Once I arrive at the mall, I can open Banjo, and it will tell me who is in the mall, where they most recently checked in, and how long ago that was. Note that I do not need to have any connection with the users to see this information. Finally, as I am waiting patiently in line to make my purchase, I open Glancee, once again to see who is around me, but this time I see someone on Glancee who has interests similar to mine. As Glancee is an opt-in service only, I know that they are likely receptive to me saying, "Hi, I was just checking out Glancee and see you are on it too. It says you like '80s music. Are you more the one-hit wonder crowd or the hair-band crowd?"

At this point, you may be on the verge of banning all social-media use in your family. I understand the reaction. The above uses are generally innocent enough, but there is far too much accessibility for creepy people to engage your teenager. There is a simple fix to this. With any check-in application, the user privacy settings are critical. When you set them to "Private" or "Share with Friends," the other applications cannot access the data that is otherwise publicly shared. Thus, if your daughter checks in at the mall, the only way a person on Banjo (or other apps like it, such as Sonar or Circle) can see that she is present is if the two of them are friends already. These applications simply grab what is shared publicly and make it available in one spot so that you know who is around you. Ideally, people who are already connected use them, but others will use them for less than "positive" means. Localmind and Glancee are opt-in services to begin with, so unless your son has an account on one of those services, he will not be approached by strange people asking about common interests. Glancee is for the world's extrovert population!

Music

Spotify
Pandora
Last.fm

What is social about music applications? All three of these sites provide users with ways to listen to music through a streaming service. Friends can connect and share music tastes, comments, and playlists with one another. Spotify is the largest selection of the three, while Pandora holds exclusive rights to major artists that the others do not yet have.

Last.fm does the best job of introducing new music from indie acts. In addition to these three platforms, IHeartRadio is owned by Clear Channel, which gives users access to hundreds of streaming radio stations and limitless "build your own" station potential. Again, users are able to share their playlists and opinions not only through these platforms but by pressing the button that posts what they are listening to on Facebook, Twitter, or Google+. It is a great way for a user to find new music and for a band or marketer to find a new audience.

Special Interests

Flixster
GetGlue
Viggle
Yap.tv
Yelp

Urbanspoon
Tumblr
Posterous
Xanga
Blogger
Wordpress

Seeing a new movie or watching your favorite TV show is almost always fun, yet some application developers are trying to make it more fun through social media platforms. By commenting, rating, and sharing, you meet new people and hear new views about thriller plot lines. Applications like Flixster, GetGlue, Viggle, and Yap.tv make this possible. While these apps specialize, many media networks like ESPN, CBS, and Disney are finding ways to create similar social engagement and content through their websites. For example, watching a basketball game on ESPN can be paired with the channel's web coverage of the game, where fans comment on the action and studio commentators add information that may not be shared on the television broadcast.

When it comes to food, no one wants to spend money on a bad dining experience. If you ever have, you tell people about it. What we want are great experiences, and we want to tell about those too. Yelp and Urbanspoon allow community members to write reviews about places they have been. Other features of the site are check-ins, cuisine searches, menus, what's nearby, photo sharing, and a rating system.

Blogs are still a resource for learning and sharing specialized content. The best bloggers find ways to engage their readership as well, encouraging comments, questions, and idea sharing. Tumblr, Posterous, Xanga, Blogger, and Wordpress are the more popular blogging platforms. Often with blogs, social media is used to raise awareness of the blog through postings on the various networks with a link to the blog. Individuals, fans, companies, and faith communities use blogs in various ways to engage their readers.

New Ideas and Design

Pinterest
LoveIt
Fancy

The best known applications for new ideas and design is Pinterest, the global phenomenon that has users pinning ideas, pictures, items for sale, and things they love to digital boards for safe storage but also for others to see. By following others' pinboards, the user is constantly given access to ideas that inspire someone else. Some of the most popular uses are sharing recipes and home organization advice, works of art, and books to read. One can find other pinners sharing information on most anything imaginable. By repinning an item to your board, it is safe in your possession for when you are ready to use the information.

Others sites are similar to Pinterest. LoveIt allows users to create private collections and provides a more streamlined view of information about the items pinned. The other major difference is that Pinterest claims copyright over things posted to the boards on their platform. That is a big deal if you are a professional artist or photographer.

Fancy is also a social collection platform. It has a beautiful interface. As you scroll over items in the stream, the site tells you how much they cost and where you can get them. Fancy also incorporates group-buying power into their site. In many ways, it is a shopping wish list, built for discovery and collection of things you "fancy."

What Social Media Is Not

Beyond these apps, social media offers hundreds of other specialty uses in which users connect and share ideas, from video gaming to dating sites. The power of social media is its access to ideas and people. In a discussion about social media, however, it is also important to consider what it is not.

Social Media Is Not a Fad

Parachute pants, pet rocks, and Beanie Babies were fads. They were never going to stay part of the culture for long. Classic chinos, pet dogs, and baby dolls, on the other hand, have staying power. How about social media? Social media fits with the latter group. It is not a fad. Particular apps and platforms may rise and fall, like Friendster, MySpace, and others before it. Many, if not all of those mentioned in this book, will have a shelf life. What will not pass away is the desire to use technology to enhance our connections and thirst for knowledge. Social media is the Web 2.0. This assumes that a 3.0 version will eventually come to the forefront. It will build on what exists and hopefully make it better. Futurists will make predictions, sometimes the crazier the better, about what digital communication will look like one day, but it is certain that social media will play a role in some shape or form, if for no other reason than the demographics of the under-forty population that is currently using social media. In 2012, Facebook exceeded 1 billion users. That is one-seventh of the world's population, accounting for 20 percent of all page clicks on the World Wide Web. Twitter is growing the fastest in the 18-29 demographic, with teenagers catching up quickly.[24] *Social media is not a fad.*

Social Media Is Not Community

Earlier in this book, we talked about the distinctions between social media and community. It is clear that social media lacks the ability to create true community. It can enhance community, but it cannot substitute for community. The greatest danger lies in is allowing ourselves to think that social media is community, which in turn isolates us. Human beings are social creatures. We are also curious creatures, often attracted to the shiniest and newest things. While novelties distract us for a time, eventually we return to the relational aspect of our humanity. God created us, saying that it is not good for us to be alone. In our curiosity, we may seek new ways to communicate, but when we recognize the absence of touch, laughter, and relationships built through proximity, we will seek to regain them. *Social media is not community.*

Teenagers need adults who are willing to discuss the distinctions between connections and true community. We facilitate such discussions in communities of faith when we designate non-tech times on retreats or at events. We teach these distinctions when we make face-to-face conversations a priority over e-mails or texts. Along with these observable actions, we need to have frank, honest talks about social media and community. As parents and ministers, we can teach our teenagers about true community, or we can hope they learn the difference for themselves. The latter is simply too risky. Talk about what social media is not with your teenagers by scheduling time together—without devices—and asking a few of these questions:

• How does it feel to be disconnected for a little while?
• What are you worried about missing?
• Why is it important to spend time together without devices?
• Who are the most important people in your life? Explain why.
• What are your dreams? What are your goals for next year at school? (Ask additional questions that help them share about themselves.)

Social media is *not* community, but it can certainly be a conduit for building community and new relationships. After many years in one city, my family moved to a new city for my wife's job. Social media fueled my attempts to network. By using Twitter, Facebook, LinkedIn, and Meetup, I was able to find local events to attend and people to meet. This would have eventually happened without social media, but I was able to accelerate the process because I knew more about the events, the organizers, and their values before attending. I was better able to connect with people I met afterward through digital means. Ultimately, though, what was critical was my focus on moving the online connections I had formed into offline relationships. I believe in the positive power of social media because I have lived it as new city resident, as a minister, as an educator, and as a community member. But the key point in the process is to turn digital relationships into real ones. We should encourage this healthy goal for our teenagers as they engage and play in the digital playground.

Social Media Is Not Always Honest

A parent named Jen shared a story after a family spring break experience. They took a short vacation to a beach a few hours from home. On the way back afterward, Jen's daughter remarked that they did not do anything fun for spring break. Jen noticed the iPhone in her daughter's hand and asked, "Have you been on Instagram?" Her daughter smiled when she realized that, rather than recognizing the fun experience her family had together, she was comparing it to the pictures friends took from more exotic locations. Jen's daughter was so envious of these other trips that she was expressing dissatisfaction about a great time she had with her family. Luckily, Jen was paying attention and able to point this out.

Earlier, I told the story about teenage girls who took a "spontaneous" Instagram photo and posted it after the fourth take. Perhaps that is planned spontaneity, but let's take this a step further. Are you aware of a condition called Facebook envy? Boston psychologist and Harvard Medical School professor Craig Malkin says he observes it in his practice with increasing frequency.

> We're really just in the infancy when it comes to this research, but there are some themes that are emerging. And one of the clearest themes is when people go on to Facebook they're often crafting a persona—they're portraying themselves at their happiest. They're often choosing events that feel best to them and they're leaving out other things.[25]

Recently, a youth ministry student in one of my classes asked a question about this topic. He wanted to know how we help teenagers who struggle with their self-esteem to recognize that what they see on Facebook is not the whole story. *Social media is not always honest.*

Before we blame this on Facebook, though, consider that generations of humans have projected their best outward image while conveniently leaving out the worst. Family photos from the 1950s hardly tell the story of war veterans dealing with what they experienced in Europe or the Pacific. Home movies from the 1960s do not reflect women's struggles as they sought their voice and power, if not for themselves then for their daughters. People dress for church, say the right things, and act like their families are perfect, but we know some screamed at each other in the car on the way, some are hiding the shame of poor decisions from the week before, and others are barely keeping their marriages together. Before we suggest that social media only projects positive parts of our lives, then, we must recognize that as human beings, that is what we are conditioned to do.

Imagine how uncomfortable it would feel to read a friend's status update about marital struggles or see a photo of a mother whose teenage daughter had to pick her up from a neighbor's party after she passed out from drinking too much. How would you respond to that transparency? The problems associated with Facebook envy come from our own feelings that everyone has a better life than we do, forgetting that they are only projecting the best parts. That couple on the romantic cruise may be there because they forgot how to love each other. That father-son trip to a Major League ballpark may be the result of the dad telling his son he has cancer. We simply do not know the stories behind the photos. Social media does not tell the full story. Does that make it dishonest? Or is this simply a function of human behavior?

Teenagers do the same thing with the pictures they post of people they are with at a party or with people on Twitter. For a learning activity at church one night, ask students to come prepared by tweeting pictures with a specific hashtag so that you can access them from your laptop (such as #therealstory). Tell them the exercise is to view the pictures and then tell the story of what is happening in them. On several occasions, they may get close, but their interpretations will probably be wrong for many of them. Debrief the activity by talking about how we see ourselves or what we often want to see in someone else's pictures. Explain that, usually, this is not even what the picture is about.

Here's a simpler version of an experiment that I tried: I posted a photo of blue flowers in a field. Personally, I thought the picture was remarkable.

The response from peers was affirming. But I showed my ten-year-old daughter the picture and she said, "Daddy, aren't those the little blue flowers in the front yard, and aren't the tall green plants in the back blades of grass?" By posting the photo and labeling it "wildflowers in a field," I created an image that people wanted to see. Would it have been as compelling with the label, "little blue-tipped weeds in my front yard"? When viewing images and engaging with others on social media, it is important to remember that the story is never completely told about the beauty, despair, or opinions expressed and experienced by the human condition.

Social Media Is Not Good or Bad

Many years ago, a colleague was convinced that the world was bad and was out to destroy our children. He implied that adults must be diligent in teaching young people to reject the world. Being steeped in postmodern culture with teenagers, I disagreed with him. I believe that teenagers need to be equipped to navigate the world and its inhabitants and effectively be the presence of Christ to both the whole and the broken. The world is neither evil nor good. Both extremes—and everything in between—exist in the world. Social media is similar in that regard.

Many people say that social media is not good. In many respects, they are right. Teenagers could be described as the head-down generation because they stare at their phones too much. Adults are too connected to work at all times through their e-mail and texts. People ignore the human beings who are physically in front of them, preferring the avatar and icon of the person sending messages or tweets. Families can sit at the same table and never say a word to one another as one updates his status, another catches up on tweets, and the rest play games with friends online. I occasionally scroll through pictures I have taken on my phone. I found one that I saved from spring the previous year. In the image, my wife, kids, and I are at a restaurant having dessert, sitting on a patio that provides a beautiful view of the city. The picture is not of the city or smiling faces, but rather of my wife checking her e-mail, my son playing Words with Friends, and my daughter playing one of her digital games. For once, I thought before I spoke, realizing that I could not say anything to them because I had my phone out to take a photo so I could post it to Facebook. I posted a photo of the city, but it showed a family lost in their screens. Social media is not necessarily good, but this incident was not social media's fault.

We could also say that social media is not bad. It is a tool that humans use—sometimes in amazing and beautiful ways. We can share inspirational words from a sermon with all of our followers in just a few seconds. We can take pictures during a mission trip that allow parents at home to feel like they are with us. We can tell hundreds of people our exciting news, prayer concerns, and everything in between with a handful of keystrokes. But we can also become disconnected, at risk, and unsafe using the same tools. Social media is not the evil trying to destroy our children and teens, but it is a means of communication that adults need to educate themselves about. In this way, we can be actively engaged as observers or participants on the playground with our teens, helping them learn the behaviors that allow them to stay safe, have fun, and build real community. We can say all the right things, but teens need to see us model these behaviors.

Social media is not good or bad. A tension exists between its good and bad possibilities. These tensions play into facets of who teens are and who they are trying to become. My friend Barrett is a youth minister who instituted a policy for weekend retreats: cell phones go into a basket when the retreat begins. At first, as you might imagine, he was met with resistance from the teens and a few adults. He described the first night as one spent with a bunch of addicts in detox. By the next morning, though, few people seemed concerned any longer. They invested in one another. They found ways to entertain themselves. He noticed their ability to immerse themselves in the contemplative worship practices of the weekend. On Sunday as they returned to the church, he gave the phones back. While a few hungrily began to consume the media, others put the phones in pockets or backpacks. This policy is now standard for his group, and he rarely hears a complaint. At multiple times, he has even heard what a relief it is to put the phones away and not feel the pressure to respond. As parents or faith leaders, what do we make of this story? Surely Barrett's teenagers are not a unique breed. To begin thinking through these questions, let's return to the playground.

The Sandbox: A Spiritual Mixture, Part 2

The digital sandbox where teenagers live and play creates unlimited opportunities for them to see, hear, and express divergent viewpoints. Many of these viewpoints provide a strong argument simply based on the ability to deconstruct parts of faith as understanding. For teenagers, this is particularly troubling in their faith formation. In and of itself, deconstruction is not bad. It involves breaking down ideas and systems into a basic point. During our teenage and college years, this is part of the critical-thinking process.

The danger comes when we do this in a vacuum that does not provide the tools, resources, or guidance to reconstruct new thoughts or rebuild beliefs. Teenagers who are exploring and expanding their faith need people to guide them through the process.

Andrew Root, professor of Youth and Family Ministry at Luther Seminary and co-author of *Theological Turn in Youth Ministry* (IVP, 2011), suggests that youth ministers think theologically about what is happening in the lives of teenagers. First, this requires paying attention to the common experience of the group or an individual at an event or in a conversation. What is happening? What is being discussed? The second part is critical: reflection and evaluation. What was significant about the event or conversation that defines the experience? What was said and why? Root suggests that ministers need to reflect both sociologically and theologically on the experience. This reflection leads to the third component, action. What do I do to teach, lead, or educate in this moment? Do I continue with plans for the Bible study on Nehemiah, or is there something else that needs greater attention?

Here is an example. Haley and Jackie were reading a *Cosmopolitan* magazine during the bus ride to our fall retreat one year. I sat in the seat across the aisle from them and asked what had their attention. After a few minutes of avoiding the topic, they finally gave in and showed me the article. The article, which discussed how to tell if a guy is lying, was framed in the context of a young, single adult woman who was trying to determine if her boyfriend was sleeping with someone else and lying to her about it. I asked if I could read the article, which I did, and then I perused the rest of the magazine. That conversation was our experience, and because I was reading *Cosmo*, it became everyone else's experience. Teenagers talk, after all. That night as I sat outside, making sure everyone stayed in their assigned rooms, I thought about that article, the content, the rest of the adult subject matter in the magazine, and the girls' interest in the "lie detector." I thought about it from the perspective of what the world is teaching them and how it differs from what the Scriptures teach about healthy relationships and body image. Next came my action. I decided to offer a voluntary chat session the next day during free time. To my surprise, a number of girls and guys came to talk rather than swim or hang out. We had a great conversation that evolved into a new common experience, which led to more reflection on my part and an eventual education series on Sunday nights.

This was a spiritual discernment process, and in the spiritual mixture of the sandbox, the faithful followers of Christ must pay attention to how teenagers are experiencing God. Teenagers are bombarded with messages from people who speak and post as authorities. They are exposed to things for which they have no answers or words to articulate their feelings. When the terrorist events of September 11, 2001, happened, many in our congregation came to church the next night to find someone who could help them with their words. Teenagers are no different, except that they do not know to ask for help or even if they need help. The job of parents and ministers is not only to provide space for the presence of God in the lives of teens but also to help them be aware of their experience with God and aid them in finding language to describe it.

Recall the "on the wall," "behind the wall," and "off the wall" language discussed in the introduction to this book, using insights from Walter Brueggeman and Kenda Creasy Dean. "Behind the wall" language gives students the faithful language to connect and cry out to God, whether with cries of despair, joy, or sighs too deep for words. These "behind the wall" words carry them far when in the presence of other people of faith, but what do they do when they experience events in which the dominant culture does not have this language? We use "off the wall" language—art, social media, or music—to communicate with the world that does not yet know Christ. My friend, who is a life coach (that is, someone who teaches others to improve their performance, deepen their learning, and otherwise enhance their quality of life) tells a story about his group that regularly meets online for web chats. These are not necessarily people of faith, but they often delve into matters of the spirit. He challenges them to use social media to remain connected between meetings, but with a purpose. Once, he asked them to post a picture on Instagram of where they saw God that week. They were not to use words. At the end of the week, they were allowed to comment on one another's images and ask questions. These photographs were "off the wall" language through which people who are not particularly faithful had the chance to experience the presence of Christ in those who are. It also created conversation on how the participants defined, understood, and related to God.

We can ask teenagers "behind the wall" language questions and use social media to teach them to share their faith through this language. A teenager who struggles with confidence issues might be asked to take photos of things that make her feel stronger. A youth group might use a Flickr page to share pictures during the week of where they see God in their daily lives. The language we use is a major component of storytelling.

Faith formation begins in young children with the stories and gestures of the church. As children get older and their ability to think more abstractly grows, they need people of faith to play alongside them in the sandbox, helping them explore, build, and tear down new castles of ideas. They need people who can rake the sand with their hands and let the questions develop into conversations that shape their faith and their sense of God around them. Youth ministers, volunteers, and parents are all capable of playing this role. My wife's favorite activity when at the beach is to find a shallow pool of water and build sand castles by letting the wet sand drip from her fingers and build upon itself. It looks like the drippings from a wax candle that melts and reforms elsewhere. Once, I watched as my son quietly observed her doing this. He eventually sat next to her and tried to build a castle of his own. After a few starts and stops in which great globs of sand destroyed his castle, and after a few tips from my wife, he was off and building his own masterpiece. Most fascinating to me was the animated conversation they had while playing in the sand next to one another. She was no longer mindlessly letting sand drip through her fingers as she read a novel, and he was no longer oriented on building some great piece of art. Instead, they were totally engaged with one another.

The relationships of volunteers, parents, and ministers to teenagers are important. We sit on retreats, van rides, at meals, in Sunday school, at work sites, and on football bleachers, and we rake the sand for our teenagers. We build relationships on common experiences and trust. As adults, you know the language of teenagers, and you know the language of the faith community. When questions about global affairs, relationship troubles, social justice causes, parents, siblings, and the future arise, you sit in the sandbox with teenagers and have the opportunity to reframe the questions they ask, challenging them to think beyond what the voices of culture say to consider what the voice of Christ says. You can reframe their questions within the context of faith. You can teach them to think with the mind of Christ so that, even when you are not able to be present in the sandbox, you can know that they are equipped to consider new information through the lens of their faith community. As we return to the playground, keep the value of such relationships in mind.

The Slide: A Slippery Place, Part 2

Have you ever watched to see how a small child learns that the slide is fun? Climbing the ladder may be too risky. Mom and Dad quietly reassure him and then place the diaper-bottomed toddler on the slide a few feet up. While holding on to the child, they let him slide to the bottom. After a few turns, the child may want to slide from a higher spot on the slide or without the parent holding him. Eventually, as confidence grows he will not only slide alone but will also scale the ladder to do so. In the first few years, though, a parent usually waits dutifully at the bottom to catch him as he slides off.

The slippery nature of our culture puts teenagers in a place where they are not always aware of the risks associated with certain behaviors. For instance, posting inappropriate photos or bullying comments online has long-term consequences, but in the moment it may seem acceptable. When left alone on the slide, teenagers sometimes make unsafe choices. They may choose to make the slide unsafe by making it faster or piling too many people on. They may try to climb the slide rather than the ladder, or jump from the side. Messages presented to teenagers and the ability to express opinions about them instantaneously through social media are slippery places. Taking a chance to be provocative or funny is not a bad thing, but who calls foul when a line is crossed? Not another teenager.

As teenagers probe and explore what it means to become adults, they say and do things that hurt other people. Often they are not even aware of it. As adults who love them, we occasionally have to deal with the times when they get hurt. And when they hurt another person, we need to be present to remind them of their claim to be the presence of Christ to others. We need to remind them of sins of diminishing others. We do this when we hear it on the phone or in our living rooms. We correct teens when they are cruel to siblings or friends. But the digital slide is another issue altogether. If we are not nearby, chances are we will not ever realize the need to be an example and teach teenagers how to hold themselves to the higher standard of God's love.

Though we might wish that a lesson learned once is enough, the reality is that it is not. As a child, I had tremendous freedom to explore my neighborhood and ride my bike to many great places. One place I was not allowed to go was across the railroad tracks behind my friend's home. According to my mother, it was an issue of safety. To me, though, the neighborhoods to be explored on the other side were magical and mysterious. After getting in trouble once for going across the tracks, I did it again. In fact, I did it many more times. I occasionally got caught and grounded, but it rarely made me stop to think about not doing it again. I stopped only after a friend got hurt riding over there and we could not get him home easily. This incident made me aware of the dangers of being where I was not supposed to be and of the consequences for the other person as well.

Even when we teach teenagers about the importance of following the example of Christ, the lessons do not always sink in. Adults are the same way. Our friends, like mine growing up, contribute to the pressure that leads us to making poor choices. Cyberbullying is made worse by the fact that people can pile on posts or comments without stopping to see the reaction of the offended party. At a conference where we presented together, Michelle Icard of Michelle in the Middle told a story. Her daughter is an Instagram super user. The two of them review her account regularly. A recurring event caught Michelle's attention. Girls were posting a grid of four pictures, numbering them, and asking the question, "Who is the prettiest? Rank by number." These Instagram beauty pageants usually devolved into a number of harsh comments from posters, often directed at the one girl in the pageant who was not likely a willing participant. That girl would read mean comment after mean comment about her appearance. This is a particularly awful form of bullying, as the original poster can claim innocence to what took place in the comment section. How do we not only keep our teenagers from participating in these situations but also teach them to be the presence of Christ in the midst of them? Is it enough to teach them to be nice to the bullied individual, or is there truth that needs to be spoken to the offenders? Teenagers need adults who can counsel them in these incidents, and, in some cases, they need to be the ones who call for bullying to stop. Some situations encountered in the digital playground are adult situations, and adults need to be aware and available to model the best ways to address them. Our teenagers should not be left alone to try to fend for themselves.

As culture accelerates the move from child to adult, teenagers increasingly need people they trust to help them navigate the passage. They need someone to challenge the messages that encourage unsafe or bad choices on the slide. They need someone to catch them as they learn to do it themselves. They may even need you to slide down a few times so they can see how it's done.

The Merry-go-round: A Head-spinning Pace, Part 2

Generation Z may be the most over-programmed generation of teenagers and children that has ever existed. The pace is dizzying. Social media gives teenagers the feeling of always being connected and in the know. It contributes to FOMO (Fear of Missing Out). Who does not want to know the latest gossip, news, or sports score? We are curious creatures that want instant access to information, and this leads us to searching for it. Load this in with the amount of activities and commitments packed into a teenager's day or week, and it might just cause information overload, or burn out. The Psalmist told his readers to "Be still." Why, just so they would not disturb him? Was it because we need rest? Was it so we could reflect on our accomplishments and prioritize our next steps? No, of course not. If you are familiar with the passage, you already know the purpose...to know God, to be in the presence of God.

Making time for Sabbath, to rest in God's peace and to exhale are very important to our spiritual formation, and to our own mental and emotional health. The farmer understood the psalmist. Sabbath means returning thanks. It means taking a day to reflect on the blessings of the Creator. It means resting in the love of community, worshipping together, re-creating together. Teenagers do not understand the need to stop, be still and know God. Each day is a 24 hour news cycle, stores are open 7 days per week and there is always work to be done. Perhaps a full day of rest is too much to expect in American culture and the global economy ever again, but daily moments of Sabbath must not be ignored.

What Sabbath looks like will probably be different for every person. A walk in the woods may be restorative for one while a nap is for another. A few moments reading scripture, moments of meditation, and staring at the clouds in the sky may be Sabbath for you, while your teenager may need time unplugged, listening to music or journaling. The stillness starts by removing the distractions. Social media can be a distraction, but only if we let it be. As teenagers race to the merry-go-round, is anyone reminding them that it is not going anywhere? Are we reminding them that it's okay for the ride to be slow rather than fast? Do we show them options for stillness on the field or on a bench beside the playground? The merry-go-round may be the most dangerous piece of equipment on the digital playground because it causes us to rush to the next, not appreciating the now or paying homage to what has been. We counteract this by reminding teenagers of the Sabbath. We celebrate rites of passage that do these things: graduation, getting their driver's licenses, birthdays, anniversaries and other significant milestone markers we call to memory. Celebrate the here and now, honor the past. The merry-go-round can wait, but you have to be willing to model it for them too. There are several ways that you can do this. Many families and youth groups have taken a social media sabbatical, anywhere from two days to two weeks. They sign a pledge to one another, announce their departure from social media for the determined time and focus on their relationships with one another and with God. Many youth groups have done this with a daily devotional book and journal that they use to document their feelings and discoveries. This is an extended Sabbath, but not all experiences need be.

Sabbath may be daily at a prescribed time or at random times. Sabbath may be moving away from social media, or we might use social media to remind people of Sabbath. One group of which I am aware uses Facebook and Instagram for their devotions and responses. Another uses it as a text messaging service that reminds everyone to be still for a few minutes. They are encouraged knowing that others in the group are doing the same thing wherever they are. Our culture does not value stillness. We are over-programmed and over-stimulated. Business is the "on the wall" language of our society. We can use the "off the wall" language and tools of social media to encourage and teach teenagers (and ourselves) the value of Sabbath. The group of people who take pictures to post and reflect upon use the "off the wall" to be still for a few moments. If people who are not self-identifying as followers of God can take a daily Sabbath, then certainly the people of God should be able to as well.

The Swing: Always a Seat for the Lonely, Part 2

Sitting on the digital swing makes a person feel like she is playing with others. Other people are doing the same actions, commenting on the same pictures, reading tweets, and posting to Facebook. Yet, sadly, they are all doing it in isolation from community. Walk past a two-year-old Sunday school or daycare class, and you might see lots of small toddlers exploring centers, playing with blocks or cars, coloring or painting, playing dress-up, or looking at books. What may look like children playing together at first glance looks different after a closer examination. The children are playing, as a teacher friend likes to tell me, "near each other." Their interactions tend to come in fast and furious flashes when one takes the crayon the other wanted, or a block tower gets knocked down before it is complete. These actions are not those of children playing together. As a similar example, when my wife was in Indianapolis a few years ago, I received a text from her saying that she was having dinner with Peyton Manning. Excited for her, I told her to sing "Rocky Top" to him (those unfamiliar with Tennessee football may not understand this reference to the game's official song in that state). Her next text said that he was actually at the table next to hers, eating with a friend. She may have been in the same restaurant as Peyton, even in the same room, but she was not eating dinner with him.

Teenagers who mistake social media for community are like the two-year-olds, my wife in Indianapolis, and the lonesome person who finds an empty swing. They might be "near" another person, but they are not building relationships. By connecting and cultivating engagement with our teenagers in the social world, we can teach them the value of balancing online connections with offline community. We may need to model it by getting them off the swing and into relationships with others over dinner or ice cream. Providing frequent opportunities for face-to-face interaction among teenagers, whether they are youth group members or your own children, is important. Model and insist that "real-life" interactions are primary. For example, you take a group of four teenagers from a youth group to get Chinese food. On the ride to the restaurant, set ground rules. No phones should be out at the table after the first two minutes. Give them time to announce to their networks that they are at lunch with their youth minister, and even take a fun photo of the group in the restaurant. After that, no texting, tweeting, posting, or liking anything in the digital world. That goes for you, the adult, as well. Some teenagers are not natural conversationalists, thus making digital interaction easier for them, but life is not fully lived behind a screen and keypad.

Teaching teenagers how to have conversations, ask good questions, and share stories is an undervalued art. It is also something we as adults can pass on to our teenagers. Jesus invested in a small crowd of followers, teaching them to love as he loved. He demonstrated a model for deep, intimate relationships and interactions. He developed the ability to be honest at levels we can only hope to attain. He showed care for the 5,000. He taught the crowds. But he knew the Twelve. Our model for our teenagers, as parents or as ministers, is to demonstrate the value of friendship, intimacy, and knowing another person. That knowing is not the knowledge gained on the FOMO ("fear of missing out") merry-go-round. It is a relationship with others who mutually care for one another. It comes from knowing God and being known by God.

The Dangers of Social Media

Left unchecked, social media can corrupt a teenager's sense of self. The online identities that teenagers develop can be authentic or false. While there is a benefit for teenagers to play with different identities or aspects of personalities, there is also a danger in not knowing who they are or, worse, pretending to be someone they are not. We learn who we are by our interactions with others, our shared experiences, and our reflections on them. That cannot happen on the digital playground. What gets created or viewed online are the identities that teenagers create for themselves, often to appeal to others rather than to be authentic. Facebook envy affirms for teens where they fit on the social hierarchy based on who is tagged in pictures with whom. It gives them a ranking in the social caste system based on who their "friends" are, who ignores their requests, and who de-friends them later.

This system for identity development is not healthy, but it is also not just a social media problem. It is a human condition where people can be ignored and made to feel "less than." Twitter does not cause this problem, but it can magnify it. When a person is ignored digitally, it feels every bit as painful as when they are ignored in real life. This occurs when teenagers are left to develop their identity in isolation from adults who are capable of seeing the beauty within their souls. The love of Christ comes from followers of Christ who love teenagers when they cannot love themselves. It comes from those who love them when they do not merit that love. The household of faith offers a unique way for teenagers to find community, wholeness, and acceptance. It offers unconditional love, grace, and mercy. If teenagers are to be part of this community, the adults who love and minister to them should be active participants in their digital lives as well as in real life, continually reinforcing the notion that the two are not separate.

Resident Aliens Revisited Digitally

Stanley Hauerwas and Will Willimon wrote *Resident Aliens* in 1989 to describe life in the Christian colony. They had a sense that something was wrong then, and, reading their words more than twenty years later, we can know that something is still amiss today. In describing how Christians are resident aliens, they wrote,

> To be resident but alien is a formula for loneliness that few of us can sustain. Indeed it is almost impossible to minister alone because our loneliness can too quickly turn into self-righteousness or self-hate. Christians can survive only by supporting one another through the countless small acts through which we tell one another *we are not alone, that God is with us.* Friendship is not, therefore, accidental to the Christian life.[26]

In this brave new world of social media, being present on the playground matters. How we minister to our teenagers and their connections through them matters. Before delving into how we do that, Hauerwas and Willimon have a few more things to say about becoming resident aliens.

The resident alien lives in a colony where one culture exists in the middle of another. Adults nurture the young to navigate the larger culture, using the distinctive traits that come from the colony.[27] There are infinite ways to segment culture and demographics, both in the physical world and the digital one. The digital playground is a new, emerging culture for which the church was not prepared. The Internet brought swift and mostly welcome innovation and change. Social media has added layers that we are still trying to understand and explain. The culture around the church and families is changing rapidly, and we have the choice to adapt our methods and understandings or to risk becoming irrelevant and unable to communicate with future generations. This is more than changing music styles or dress codes. It is more than sitting in padded chairs rather than pews or meeting in an auditorium versus a sanctuary. Adapting our methods to relate to a changing culture means recognizing that we live in a post-Christian society. It means realizing that the "on the wall" language is changing, as are tools for communicating. While we continue to practice communicating the gospel in the ways that worked in the 1950s, our young people will look for those who speak a language that makes sense to them. In turn, they lose the ability to be nurtured in tenets of faith that remind them that they are different— they are claimed by God. Many adults struggle with understanding the claim God has placed on us at our baptism, so imagine how difficult it will be for teenagers to understand that if they are not given language and nurture within the Christian household of faith.

Throughout history, the church has been known to wait until it was too late. Whether in response to politics, war, slavery, or human rights, the church has been slow. Then it reacts with efforts to catch up, often too late. In 1995's *Purpose Driven Church*, Rick Warren wrote about churches where we listened to an oratory speech, sang along with pipe organs, and sat on wooden pews. These are hundreds-of-years-old methods of telling and responding to a story. We accept them in the church but would never consider them as viable ways to sell products at work, engage with a story at the movie theater, or sit for meaningful conversation with another person. Social media has the church playing catch-up again. The difficulty this time is not only about catching up to the digital culture but catching up to fourteen-year-olds who have grown up with devices and screens in their hands. As people of faith, we cannot rely on an app to teach our children and teenagers about faith and God's presence in the world. That is both something to fear . . . and to celebrate.

It is fearful because we have to find new ways to teach and to learn. We have to find fresh ways to share the gospel on the new playground. It is worth celebrating because the message has not changed. As people still feel the pull of God, we should make space for them to respond. Our faith calls us to be engaged with the world around us, and it calls us to engage the world differently, politically and socially. As the world is shifting and changing, expanding and shrinking, the church has a fantastic opportunity to effect change in it through our teenagers whom we love and the adults they will become.

As we try to make sense of social media, our use of it, our teenagers' use of it, and how to create balance and boundary, we have to be conscious of the constant struggle to be in the world and not of it. The faith of which we are a part has its own playground. It is one of symbols, rites, gestures, and sacraments. Each sacrament teaches us a lesson that we can teach our teenagers about how we are different as people of faith, and how this shapes our engagement with the world and the digital playground.

Lessons from Baptism

Our baptism symbolizes the moment when God claims us. It is our public expression of belonging to God. When we join the household of faith, our lives are to become different. Micah called the Israelites to do justice, love mercy, and walk humbly with God (Mic 6:8). Jesus said to go and make disciples (Matt 28:20). The expression of the church during baptism is of welcoming the new believer but also committing to walk, learn, and serve alongside him or her. The newness of life for the Christian is one that calls the person and their faith community to be different.

If we are people of God, this extends to all aspects of our lives. Social media is not to be ignored. The lesson for us is that we are called and committed to be Christ's presence throughout the world, including on the digital playground. We are also called to model and instruct young people in living out their faith. One way we can do this is through the liturgy of the church as addressed in the next chapter.

Chapter 4

Having a Conversation about Social Media

"When I was your age, *I* was the remote control. I was excited when Atari came out and grateful for cordless phones. You kids today don't know how good you've got it."

I have yet to say anything that blatantly nostalgic to my kids, but I do think it sometimes when they complain that the batteries don't work in the remote or that they "need" a new Wii game. Nostalgia is actually fun and useful for talking about how communication has changed, even with your teens. Be self-deprecating, and watch them engage with you. Just remember that your nostalgia forgets both the complications and the benefits each new technology introduced into your own teen years. Regardless of the advances, the power of relationships between parents and teens never changes.

The primary and formative relationships for children are parental. As they enter adolescence, teens are more likely to expand their circle of influences, seeking the input of their peers as often or more than that of their parents. Seeking the opinions of friends does not mean replacing the parental influence; it means giving parents a different role. We do well to accept this role, because it will continue changing as our kids mature into adulthood. In this chapter, we explore ways that parents can have a healthier influence on teenagers' social media habits. By understanding and using social media as another method of communication in your relationship with your teen—rather than avoiding it—you can increase the scope of your influence.

The first section of this chapter is about how parents (or ministers) influence teenagers. By understanding both the positives and pitfalls of social media, you can make informed decisions that help teenagers be smarter and safer in their social media usage. The next section focuses on the importance of moving online conversations to offline relationships. As a parent, you can employ the information you view online in healthy, constructive, face-to-face conversations with your teen. The final section focuses on creating a foundation for using social media. I offer a guide for how you and your teenager can create a mutually beneficial contract that addresses your concerns about seeing one another on social media and creates expectations for how you will communicate about what you see.

A Parent's Influence

If you can recall your time as a teenager, you may remember how desperate you were not to be under the control of your parents. You needed to stretch your wings. In the 1980s, a whole genre of music, led by the Beastie Boys and Twisted Sister, had teenagers calling for their right to party as they also vowed not to take "it" anymore. That experience has been no different for teenagers of the '50s, '60s, '70s, '90s, and today. Conveniently, we remember our rebellious days without recalling how much our parents still influenced us. As a teenager, I truly feared only one person. It was neither the stereotypical bully nor the teacher who had been teaching calculus since my parents were in high school.

No, I was afraid of a 5-foot-3-inch ball of mothering. My mother wielded great power in our home. Part of my fear involved the retributive justice that occasionally came my way. As I moved into adolescence, though, that fear changed. While I occasionally worried about getting caught doing something I probably shouldn't have done, the greater fear was disappointing her and losing her trust. My mother allowed me to become the person I was growing into without a tyrannical hand, and because she did, our communication was strong. I did not want to jeopardize it. Of course, I also did not want to lose my license or car. I relied heavily on my mother for advice, and her opinion mattered because she also trusted me as I made decisions. I suspect that my experience is not unique.

My mother taught me the stories of faith. She modeled faithful living on Monday as well as Sunday. She taught Sunday school and chaperoned youth trips. To suggest that the church was the primary influence on my spiritual formation would be wrong. The church played a tremendous role in that process, but it supported what my mother was already doing. Parents are the primary role models and educators for their children and teens. That is true from etiquette training to physical care to spiritual formation. It is true on the real playground and on the digital one.

Despite a new generation of music, teenagers today still rely on their parents for advice and guidance. Teens indicate that they receive both solicited and unsolicited advice from their parents about using the Internet. Despite the fact that they seek input from a vast set of sources—friends,

Google, and others—teenagers still trust their parents for the best advice. This is why it is critical for parents to be informed. A friend recently shared that she had signed up for Instagram. She was astounded when I told her that I already knew she had signed up. My settings allow Instagram to notify me when a Facebook friend creates an account. It also tells me the person's username so I can follow his or her photo exploits on Instagram. After getting over the shock of that information, she shared that her seventeen-year-old daughter was planning to teach her about Instagram later that day. I think this is commendable!

Parents need to have a cursory understanding of the social media landscape. This does not mean you need to understand the ins and outs of every platform, but you should at least know enough about them to understand their purpose. The old adage that "information is power" rings true. Its inverse is still true as well. When you are ignorant, the power lies elsewhere. You don't ignore the changes in your teen's behavior when new friends enter her life, so don't ignore her online behavior either. Having an informed conversation at least gives you credibility and is more likely to create new opportunities for you to learn from your teenager. If you are like my friend, you might find a way to spend valuable time with your teenager as she teaches you how to use a platform like Instagram. The goal is not so much that you become an Instagram pro as that you spend time offline with your teenager.

You may be uncertain of what types of conversations to have with teenagers about their online practices. I encourage commonsense parenting in this case. Talk about what we should or should not share online. Talk about how to use cell phones and mobile social media safely. Talk about how we treat others online. Cyberbullying is real. It is just as painful online as it is face-to-face. Talk about the family matters that you do not want discussed or shared online. I saw a recent exchange where a teenager vented about his parents on Twitter. To say the least, the information was not flattering. Unfortunately, this teenager has followers on his account who know or know of his parents, and his words created an unflattering image. While venting is normal, unless this teen later posts that the situation has improved, the people who read his post may not know that his parents are, in fact, good people.

Teenagers will make mistakes using social media. If adults fail to interact, then both the frequency and the magnitude of mistakes will rise. As parents, we take proactive stances with many things in order to keep our children safe, healthy, and aware of good practices—from immunizations to driving tests. Social media and Internet use is no different. Your teenager is counting on you to provide good advice. She is in the spiritual sandbox and is calling for your guidance and opinion. Are you there to hear her? She trusts your opinion, even if she does not always agree with it. Your involvement with her social media life causes her to think and to reassess what she sees and hears.

A Ministry's Influence

The Christian education practices of a church can teach lessons about social media. Liturgical practices are one place to begin. In this section, we look at the practice of the Eucharist, when we come to the Communion table. Then we look to Advent and Lent as ways to examine how we are the presence of Christ online and how these seasons counter the messages of contemporary culture.

Lessons from the Table

The Communion Table requires us to remember Jesus' actions on the cross. We celebrate the Lord's Supper in community, not in isolation. The community is critical. This Table is where we celebrate and remember. Our celebration comes from knowing that the story does not end at the cross. The Lord's Table is a sacred place where we come together and remember. Two lessons of the Table are to remember and to be together in community. When we come to the Table, we hear the words of Jesus from his last night with the disciples: "Do this in remembrance of me." When we leave the Table, we are reminded to live our lives worthy of the sacrifice that was made for each of us. As we feed the hungry, clothe the poor, and share God's love, we do it in remembrance of Christ and his call to each of us.

In the Baptist tradition, the cup and the bread are passed from one member to the next. This act requires proximity and service to one another. We pass a plate to the person next to us. Communion is not the action of an individual. We remember the Christ collectively. The bread and the cup are a covenant in which we participate with the Body of Christ.

In the home, the table is where we gather to celebrate meals and share stories. It is where we learn our history, celebrate our blessings, and remember our sufferings. It is where we renew our bodies for the day ahead at breakfast and where we find the comfort of returning home. The table is where we have our hard conversations, do our homework, and work out problems through face-to-face communication. We are not at the table alone. Social media is a table discussion. We need to talk with our teens at the table about what we have seen and heard online. We need to talk about expectations and telling the truth. We should talk about authenticity and remembering whose we are.

The Lord's Table reminds us of whose we are in the kingdom, and the family table at home should reinforce that as we reflect of our faith together as families. The family table reminds us of whose we are on this earth. The conversations families have about social media in this context are important. It is where we set expectations, monitor them, and review them. As parents, it is where we remind our teenagers that what they post is every bit as important as what they say. How they treat others or allow others to be treated in the digital world is just as meaningful as it is in person. The family table is also where we talk about being in this digital space together. We create a covenant for how to represent ourselves and our family. It is an opportunity to remind each other daily that we are walking this new path together. If you use the questions in "Creating a Foundation for Using Social Media Together" (see below) to create a covenant, review it at the family table from time to time. Your teenagers may gripe and complain, but in the end they will be thankful that you care enough to remind them.

Lessons from Advent

Consumerism tells us that we can have what we want when we want it. This attitude is sold to teenagers, and adults are just as susceptible. Social media provides it. We get information when we want it through our phones or computers. We can talk, chat, message, and respond in an instant. There is no need to wait on the mail or to check messages when we get home. We have everything we need—information, access, and communication—in the palm of our hand. But it is never enough. We consume and consume but still thirst for more.

The season of Advent challenges us to think differently. During Advent, we wait and prepare. We wait on the child who will change the world. We prepare to celebrate. The celebration is muted because the child arrives unceremoniously in a stable. There are no tweets to announce it. The magi did not check in on Foursquare. The shepherds posted no pictures to Instagram or Facebook. When we approach social media and the digital information age with our teenagers, we should keep the lessons of Advent in our conversation.

Waiting and preparing during Advent can cultivate a spirit of patience the rest of the year. During the Advent season, churches celebrate each of the four Sundays and make preparations for the arrival of the Christ child. There is no instant gratification. If you walk patiently through the days of the season, you know what is coming, and there is no fear of missing out. Advent reminds us to wait. The old adage is that good things come to those who wait, and yet we often rush to get the next piece of information or the next hot item. We are not particularly good at waiting. Modern culture tells us we do not need to wait, but the Scriptures tell us otherwise. We are also told that there is living water that will keep us from thirsting any longer. How do we make these lessons a part of our conversation about social media? From a ministry perspective, we teach joy and peace in waiting. We highlight the moments that are captured because we are patient, rather than what we would have missed with our heads down, staring at our devices.

Teenagers need opportunities to slow down and reflect. Advent provides that. One friend's youth group uses Advent as a time to come together on Sunday nights, spending half their time in quiet reflection and journaling. Someone may read Scripture and they may sing a song, but there is no program and no pressure to produce anything. The group is there just to *be*. The last portion of the evening is a time to reflect on what they are learning about themselves during Advent. The teenagers give positive feedback about this experience, perhaps because it is the only time during the year when they are not pressured to produce posts, be online, or respond to digital messages. They are simply quiet with their thoughts and meditations, along with the Spirit of God.

Lessons from Lent

Lent offers a painful story for modern Americans. In our culture, in addition to hearing that we do not have to wait, we also hear that we do not need to sacrifice. We think we can have the proverbial cake, eat it, and eat it *now*. During the season of Lent, however, weeks of sacrifice cause us to reflect on the darkness that is Good Friday.

Social media requires no sacrifice of information or connections. Because of this, families must set limits. Those limits may differ for each family, but they are important nonetheless and should be decided intentionally. Sacrificing is not always about denying something. In the sacrifice, we often discover something we have been missing. By limiting our consumption of sugary foods, we find new energy. By limiting our financial spending on material items, we find more money and time to devote to experiences. By limiting our time on social media, we find deeper relationships sitting across the table from us.

Teaching students to limit their screen time is difficult. Remember that social media is information, and information is important in the social world of teenagers. But Lent is about limits and sacrifices. Our teenagers may make the Lenten sacrifice of avoiding chocolate or sodas during the season. Adults may do something similar. While these and other sacrifices are helpful, it might also be good to offer teenagers challenges to discover new things amid their sacrifices. Asking a teenager to give up social media during Lent will not likely pay many dividends, but what about asking them to add time with friends, family, or in personal reflection without using a device? Ask them to reflect on what they gained as a result of the sacrifice.

For parents who struggle to limit the time their teenagers spend on devices, particularly mobile ones, the challenge is even greater. While there are ways to limit smartphones, teenagers often find a way to work around the limitations. Hard and fast rules may apply for when to put devices down in the evening, but the act of limiting usage during the day is nearly impossible to achieve. Reinforcing the value of relationships and not sacrificing opportunities to engage those who are physically in our presence is a lesson worth teaching regularly. Teenagers will use their phones and social media platforms with some consistency, but when I am with them, I ask that they pay more attention to me than to those who are not present in the room. I give them the same respect. As parents and ministers, sometimes we simply need to be clear about our expectations when we are with teenagers.

Online to Offline

Throughout this book, I have mentioned the importance of allowing social media to create conversations not just online but also offline. As much as I enjoy sharing information, learning from others, and the occasional snarky comment about someone's photograph, none of this comes close to sitting down and talking with a friend over a cup of coffee. I have used social media to make contacts, keep up with friends, and as a vehicle for education. In this way, when I sit down with a new contact or with an old friend, we have a mutual jumping-off point for our conversation.

Teenagers love sharing with each other. They "like" and comment on Facebook posts. They "favorite" each other's tweets and "smiley-face" each other's pictures. They send text messages and chat online. This would lead you to believe that social media is the way they prefer to communicate. The truth is, though, that teenagers still prefer talking to each other, although texting quickly gaining ground over talking on the phone. A 2012 study by Common Sense found that teens prefer face-to-face communication to all other forms. It outpaced texting 49 percent to 33 percent because it is more fun and provides better understanding about what is communicated. It is also wise to pay attention to statistics from teenagers about their parents' media usage. Of parents who have a mobile device, many teens describe their parents as "addicted" to it.[28] In recent months, I have talked to teens who express a desire for their parents to spend less time on their iPhones and Blackberrys at dinner. Have you considered that your teenager may be thinking that, or that his or her actions may model yours? I have.

The 1950s version of the nuclear family, if it was ever true, creates nostalgia for a time when families always ate dinner together, discussed their days, and concluded the meal with thoughtful wisdom from Dad. While some families today strive to have dinner together regularly, two obstacles often arise. The first is busyness. We have a calendar in our pantry that has lines for each individual's activities and also for family commitments. While the schedule looks insane at times, ours is neither unusual nor nearly as complicated as that of many families I know. The second obstacle is the presence of technology at the table. When out for dinner, it is not unusual to see Mom, Dad, and the children using some sort of technology—whether checking e-mail, rating a restaurant, or playing a game.

If the reality in your household is that you are not together until 8:00 at night, shift how you use that time. Take advantage of the information you have seen in the public digital spaces to ask specifics about each person's day. Make these times part of your daily routine, where you check in offline with one another. Social media contributions you may have read allow you to ask direct questions about your teenager's day. Pay attention to the emotions behind the posts you have read, and decide where you want or need to dig deeper. Ask questions about how your teen's faith informs her opinion or response to situations you read about. You may be the only one asking such questions on a regular basis. Remember that you are the primary influence, even as teens look to their friends. By asking the questions no one else thinks to ask, you are making a huge impression on your teen about his value to you and the importance of letting faith inform his ethic. If the devices get in the way of face-to-face conversations, place a moratorium on them for thirty to sixty minutes so that you can catch up with each other without interruption. And as parents, take care to follow your own rules.

Rather than making social media usage a battleground with your teenager, employ it as a tool that presents opportunities to share, learn, and facilitate deeper conversations. The Shoemakers have two kids out of college and two still enrolled. For several years now, the six family members have been active on Twitter. I follow all six of them, and the interaction is incredible. There are random comments to one another, pictures shared, and links to pass along. The family is politically minded, so during presidential debates they have a running commentary with one another and with other followers in their streams. Despite being spread across multiple states and cities, the family is always in touch. But Twitter is not the only way they communicate. It simply keeps them constantly in touch. They still have meaningful conversations in person or on the phone.

Why do many teens and parents fight over social media? The reasons are varied, but they often fall into one of a few buckets. One is the escape bucket: teenagers seek to hide from their parents. A second is the fear bucket: parents latch on to the worst-case scenarios presented in the media that perpetuate old parenting fears in a new, lesser-known digital world. When fear is the primary driver, overreactions occur. This is another important reason for parents to understand social media, experience it, and then make determinations about how and what they perceive as healthy use by their teenagers. Reading fear reports from news agencies seeking page views is probably not the best way to determine the rules in your home. It is likely that fear-based prohibitions may drive teens to hide their media usage from you, creating a greater obstacle for healthy communication.

Teenagers are social creatures, just as their parents are. All humans are curious and like to know about the latest events. Teenagers know that social media is not a replacement for real-life relationships. They get frustrated when their friends, or their parents, pay more attention to texting or social networks rather than what is happening in the room with real people. They know that their own media usage can distract them from the events happening around them. The tools are great and fun, but ask one hundred teenagers where memories happen. The answers won't be from Facebook, Twitter, or Foursquare. The answers will relate to events that happen in person. Social media might capture and share the moment, but it cannot create the moment.

Creating a Foundation for Using Social Media Together

A parent told me that she did not want her daughter to get a Facebook account. It was not that she was fearful of Facebook; instead, she said that

Facebook was where she, the mom, communicates with her friends. She did not want her daughter to impinge upon her space. Everyone has a desire for autonomy and privacy. Of course, many teenagers express a similar sentiment about parents participating in social media lives. I think it is great that many parents and teenagers see eye to eye on this issue. What can they do about it? I suggest making a covenant (or an agreement, contract, compact, promise, or pledge) together (see appendix for a sample). The goal is to create a mutually beneficial contract that addresses your concerns about seeing one another on social media and establishes expectations for how you will communicate about what you see. In creating the contract together, you have the opportunity to engage your teenager about your concerns and desires for making social media a part of your relationship. Your teenager can also express concerns about your presence in her digital life, and you can address them.

A covenant provides parameters for your relationship through social media and manages the expectations of both parent and teenager. Teenagers deserve to know your parameters and concerns regarding social media. They should know what you think is acceptable behavior. They should also know that you will raise concerns when you see a problem. They should know how far you will "invade their privacy" in order to do these things. As a parent, you should know what your teenager can and can't control when it comes to the posts of their friends. You should know how much your teenager wants or doesn't want you to comment online about things they or their friends post.

It is essential to establish your concerns and expectations before an issue arises. If you do this, emotions are less likely to be involved. Also, keep in mind that certain situations may require you to reevaluate or amend the covenant. In those cases as well, try to have a conversation about them without personal attack or emotionally charged behavior. I once talked to a parent whose son had called from a party. The under-aged son had been drinking, and so had his ride. He made the right call for his dad to come pick him up. Dad made the right call to have a conversation about underage drinking the next day rather than that night. He was able to affirm his son's good decision to call while also discussing the bad decision of drinking. They had already arranged a deal if this situation ever arose: namely that the parents would wait until the next morning to discuss it. The son was safe because he had comfort knowing that his dad was not going to berate or embarrass him at the party, during the ride home, or when they arrived at home. This conversation was productive because an angry parent let his emotions cool until the next morning. Issues will arise, and predetermined expectations of how they will be handled are better for everyone. Social media is about a social identity and perception. Teenagers deserve space to make that happen. Parents deserve the right to monitor it as well.

What you put in a covenant is up to you. Your family and values are different from other families, just as your teenagers are different. Here are a few items that will help you start developing your covenant. Working with your young person, address the issues and the related questions. Decide together how you will handle them.

Safety

Your teenager may connect online with people to whom you would not want them connected in real life. Parents should be diligent to monitor friend lists and interactions that may occur with unknown people. Services like www.uknowkids.com provide social media monitoring that keeps parents informed of words associated with risky behavior or potential red-flag interactions. If you choose a service like this, make sure your teenagers are part of the process. This keeps them accountable, provides some relief for them, and gives you greater peace of mind. One example comes from a friend, Hannah, who tells the story of her son having interactions with his best friend, whom he knew was being bullied. Because the service flagged the conversation, Hannah, her son, the friend, and the friend's parents were able to address a situation that was becoming increasingly difficult for the young man to handle. Hannah's son knew that his mom was present.

With or without a service for monitoring, parents should conduct regular audits to look for unusual interactions. If your teenager is communicating with someone you do not know, ask questions about that person. If you feel comfortable with the connection, rest easy. Teenagers at camps, concerts, and extracurricular activities often connect with new people. Pay attention to these new connections and encourage the good in addition to being concerned about the bad. Brad met several new friends at a youth camp because they were all tweeting about the camp, using the camp's hashtag (#). In this context they began seeking one another, and new friendships were formed. Brad's parents asked him about the new people when he got home, but since he knew that his parents followed him on Twitter, he was not offended by their questions and happy to tell his parents about the new people he met.

One of the primary jobs of parents, after all, is keeping our children safe from physical and emotional harm. Social media has safety concerns. While they are often greatly exaggerated in the news media, the concerns still exist. To dismiss them is irresponsible. Safety is a necessary component of your social media covenant.

• What practices are we comfortable with, and which ones concern us?
• How will we address these issues when they arise?
• What privacy settings could we put in place on the social media platforms?
• How will we communicate that someone or something is making us uncomfortable on social media?

Privacy

The issue of privacy is related to safety, but it is tougher to address. As a parent, you can give an edict: "I pay for the computer (or phone), and I will see everything I want to see." If you take this stance, however, I can guarantee that you will not see it all, nor will your teenager come to you when he needs help because he will fear getting in trouble. Just as lies build on one another, so do mistakes. And even if you don't issue an edict, your teen will push back on privacy at every turn. Most, though, will accept your presence in their accounts if you establish an understanding of why it is important and assure them that you will not use the information as evidence against them. You may see things that concern you, and you will need a way to talk with your teenager about them. Your main role regarding privacy is to help your teen navigate social media safely.

My friend Lisa has a story to illustrate this point. Her fourteen-year-old daughter is active on Facebook, just like Lisa and her husband. One of their family rules and expectations is that Lisa keeps the daughter's log-in information (username, password, etc.). Periodically, Lisa examines her daughter's account, looking for red flags. One day, she found one. A person with a generic male name had "friended" her daughter, who accepted the friendship because this person was already friends with many of her other friends. The person had no picture associated with his name and had recently communicated with her daughter through private messaging. Lisa later found out that he had used the chat feature as well. Since Lisa had never heard her daughter mention this person, she clicked on his account. It listed an out-of-state location, all of his friends were young high school-aged girls, and there was no other information about him. Lisa's daughter assumed that this was someone from school because he was "friends" with her friends. She had not done anything wrong. Her mother noticed because she is diligent, and she reported the account to Facebook. The company has since removed the stranger's account. Lisa was able to have a conversation with her daughter about being more cautious in her online interactions. Unfortunately, her daughter had to grow up a little that day, losing some of her innocence. But that is a small price to pay versus the more extreme possible outcomes. In the "privacy" section of your covenant, address these topics with your teenager:

- Why does privacy invasion matter?
- How can we conduct privacy scans? Should we do this together, or should a parent do this randomly?
- What should we look for during these scans (e.g., suspicious names or locations, unsolicited contact from strangers, etc.)?
- How do we keep track of passwords and other log-in information?

Family Online Interaction

Do you remember the kid in middle school whose mom rolled down the car window on the first day of school and yelled, "I love you, Pumpkin!" Were you, in fact, that kid? He never wore orange a day of his middle school life for fear of invoking calls of "Pumpkin!" You can probably imagine similar incidents in the digital lives of teenagers. A mother posts how sweet it was that her son cuddled on the sofa with her, and she tags him in the post. Now all of his varsity football teammates see the image and her comment in their feed. A daughter posts that she is not looking forward to cleaning her room, only to find a comment from Mom that maybe she'll find that note from "x" boy she likes. Now everyone at school knows she likes him too.

Most teenagers fear humiliation, and the possibilities from parents on social media are limitless. I have had multiple conversations with teenagers who "unfriended" their parents on Facebook after Mom kept commenting on conversations she was having with friends, or blocked them on Twitter because Dad kept correcting the spelling in the tweets.

In the contract, it is important to outline how you will interact online together. Here are a few questions to get you started:

- Will you just be keeping track of how their day is going or commenting on it?
- Just how much will you comment, post, or share with them in the digital public?
- Will you engage his friends in conversation?
- Will you send friend requests to all of her friends or follow them too?
- What is "out of bounds" for interaction in the digital public?
- How late is too late to be texting or receiving texts?

When We Use Social Media

Parents often complain about the amount of time their children spend on screens, whether television, computers, phones, or video games. With smartphones, laptops, and tablets, the ease of usability has only increased. Today, I am writing on my laptop, watching my Twitter stream on my iPad, and listening to music and responding to texts on my iPhone. My son comes in, and the first thing he does after homework is hop online. My daughter wants to play games on my iPad. Managing this can be a nightmare. Imagine how difficult it is from your child's perspective when rules emerge and change based on how you feel at the moment. For example, if we allowed him to, our son would be on a screen from the time he gets in from school until bedtime. So we instituted limits. The only time this becomes a problem is if we get careless about enforcing the limits. If we do that, he has a legitimate case about mixed messages the next time I remind him of the rules.

In order to help with this, make the amount of time you spend online a part of your contract, and expect your teens to be responsible for self-policing as well.

- How will we define and measure time online? Is checking Pinterest, Instagram, or Twitter considered online time versus chatting through Facebook?
- What constitutes too much screen time?
- What is our rule about using mobile devices when we are out together as a family?

Where We Use Social Media

This heading is a subset of safety and privacy, but it bears its own space for additional reasons. It is true that privacy settings for location-based applications allow a lot of information to be shared about where we are and how often we visit each place. This can be a safety concern for parents, so it's wise to talk about it with your teenagers.

Additionally, considering where you use social media is important because of the norms of particular locations or people. Some adults may not understand a teenager's need to tweet while at a ballgame or a play. Worship services at houses of faith may not be the best time and place to stand up and take a picture of the family in the pew, then tag it in Foursquare. Negotiate some of these questions in your conversation.

• Is it appropriate to use social media mobile apps at certain family events or around certain family members?
• Are there places or times when it is less appropriate to share?
• Do we know who can see where we are when we check in at various locations?
• Where are our favorite places to post from?
• Are friends and their parents okay with being tagged at a location?

Decorum

Our neighbors have a pet pig and eight chickens. When they are out of town, they sometimes ask my daughter to feed the animals. One night during dinner, it occurred to my son that we should take staged pictures of the animals. The crown jewel of his idea was to wrap the pig in a quilt and title it "Pig in a Blanket." Hilarious, right? Not to the neighbors. It appears that my daughter thought the idea was funny enough to share with them. Now we have a rule about our dinnertime conversations: "What is said at dinner stays at dinner."

Oversharing is a common issue for new users of social media. Most new users follow a four-stage life cycle. The first stage is signing up and experimenting. For example, you finally decide to create an Instagram account. At first you try a few pictures and decide it is okay, so you add a few friend accounts to follow. Stage 2 is when you begin using the application frequently. You share photos and comments at an alarming rate. You cannot help yourself, checking multiple times per day to see what is new, what you might have missed, or how people are responding to what you've posted. At this point, you might be called an "oversharer." Some people might even choose to block you because you share too much. (The application Foursquare actually awards an "Overshare" badge! For ten-plus check-ins in under twelve hours, users get the badge.) After that wears off, stage 3 is a rejection of the application. You realize that Instagram is getting too much of your attention, causing you more stress and feelings of obligation than pleasure. You set it aside. Stage 4 is when you decide what your relationship with Instagram will be. Are you completely done with it? Are you ready to use it in a healthier, less addictive way? In this stage you settle into the pattern that will work best for you, where you are putting social media to work for you, affecting it rather than having it affect you.

There are two main types of oversharing: content and volume. We can share information that has sensitive content and should only be known to a few people. We can also post way too many thoughts and images and annoy readers with our volume. These two areas deserve consideration when negotiating a contract with your teenager. Consider the following questions to get started.

- How much sharing is too much sharing?
- What topics should we not discuss or mention through social media?
- What is the best way to engage other users?
- How is our engagement with others respectful? How do we keep it that way?
- How will we deal with cyberbullying?
- How will we make sure that we are not engaged in cyberbullying?

Areas of Concern

It is inevitable that you will see content that you do not approve of on various levels. The content may be created or shared by your teenager or one of her friends. How will you handle that conversation? What warrants a response, and what do you allow to pass? Only you, as a parent, can make this choice. My advice is to choose your battles wisely. Consider these questions together:

- What kind of online content constitutes a major concern?
- What is the best way for us to discuss it together—parent to teen?
- What might be the consequences if it keeps happening?

Connecting with Teens through Social Media

Through understanding social media and negotiating its use within your family, you will have a better foundation to use it for your benefit. Clearly, an informed and connected parent on social media is more likely to experience potential conflicts with his or her teenager. That's okay; conflict will happen either way. I believe that the pros of safety and communication far outweigh the potential conflicts. Again, each teenager will respond differently. Many teenagers will consider it normal that their parents follow their social media, while others will push back hard against it. The key is to lay a strong foundation so that you can use social media to enhance communication, not as a tool to gather evidence that you will later use against your child. The contract can lay a strong foundation, but it is for you to negotiate *together*. The one provided in the appendix is merely a sample. Yours will be unique to your family.

By paying attention to your teenager's social media sharing, likes, and posts, you can learn a lot about him, his emerging interests, his opinions, and his friends. danah boyd shares this story about a parent:

> Parent-teen communication on social network sites can enhance already healthy relationships by introducing new moments of dialogue. In Los Angeles, I talked with a father of a 16-year-old girl who was overjoyed when his daughter invited him to join her on MySpace. He saw this as a signal that he was doing something right as a parent. Through MySpace, he was able to learn things about her tastes, interests, and priorities that he did not know. At the same time, he struggled to make sense of signals that worried him. Upset by a personality quiz that suggested drug use, he carefully confronted her; she helped put the reference into context and reassured him that she had no interest in drugs. Always nervous about approaching this topic because of his own past, he valued the way that MySpace eased his ability to do so. Although father and daughter were already close, MySpace further strengthened their relationship and gave them a new channel with which to joke with one another.[29]

Several good things happened in this story that exemplify healthy communication. The first is what the father was able to learn about his daughter. He was able to ask her about these things and facilitate a time of sharing together. For example, if she mentioned her interest in an artist who was coming to their town, her father could learn about the artist and then purchase tickets for the show. The second good thing was the father's recognition of a red flag. Rather than confronting his daughter with evidence that she was a drug user, they had a conversation about a personality quiz that led to a deeper conversation about his concerns of drug use. Their connection gave him the opportunity to ease into a conversation that revolved around his own past struggles. Finally, they used this platform to continue their relationship, joking and sharing information with each other.

Teenagers still favor communicating with their parents in person. The fact that you are able to increase the topics of conversation based on your social media relationships is of great value. Your relationship with your child is best suited to face-to-face interaction, not a series of text messages or Facebook posts. The latter are tools to enhance the former. In addition everything you negotiate in your social media contract, consider the best ways for you and your teenager to approach the things that you see and learn from one another. Like all relationships, this is a two-way street. You can see their stuff, and they can see yours. What might they learn about you from your own posts and images?

You may go through a period of "overlearning" rather than oversharing. You might ask too many questions or come across as forcing conversation. Ask your teenager to help you know when too much is too much. You will figure it out. Trust your parenting instincts. Social media is a new arena, but commonsense parenting goes a long way toward navigating its use with your teenager.

Now What?

To get you started on the journey of online awareness and offline presence, here are a few tips.

1. Begin with conversation. The questions found in the section about creating a covenant (see "Creating a Foundation for Using Social Media Together" earlier in this chapter) are a place to start. You may even wish to begin drafting your covenant as you talk.
2. Start with one or two unfamiliar social media platforms. You do not need to become a super user, but get comfortable with how you see people using it and how your teenager might use it.
3. Get on the digital playground. Pay attention to the applications and platforms that your teenagers are using.
4. If safety and privacy are major concerns for you, enlist help. Caution: some people and companies use fear as a motivator to sell you unnecessary products and stalker software. Most teenagers are using social media in responsible, fun ways. There are those who use it for other means, and that bears consideration, but conversation and transparency help a family make sense of how social media will work for them.

5. Do not be afraid to ask about the things you see on social media. Your teenagers are putting information into the public domain, knowing that you or other adults will see it. Pay attention, as they may be asking you for help or may not realize they are in need of it.

6. Keep everything in perspective and pick your battles.

7. Start a parent group at your church where you can talk about social media, parenting, and issues of spiritual formation. All three are great topics for parents. Sharing joys, frustrations, prayers, and gratitude not only affirm you but also remind you that you are all committed to loving and shaping the teenagers in your faith community. It always feels better to know that you are not alone.

8. Friend, like, tweet, plus, and share on!

Notes

1. Walter Brueggemann, *Interpretation and Obedience: From Faithful Reading to Faithful Living* (Minneapolis: Fortress Press, 1991) 50–51.

2. Kenda Creasy Dean, "Healthy Congregations and Young People: What the Faith of Our Teenagers Is Telling the American Church," PowerPoint slide lecture from Churchworks conference, 26 February 2013, Ft. Worth TX.

3. "Discovery Forum Statistics," Institute for Emerging Issues, North Caroline State University, Raleigh, 2012, http://iei.ncsu.edu/wp-content/uploads/2013/01/ForumPaperFinal_2_2-41.pdf.

4. Common Sense Media, "Social Media, Social Life: How Teens View Their Digital Lives," 2012, http://www.commonsensemedia.org/research/social-media-social-life (accessed 10 August 2012).

5. danah boyd, "Why Youth (Heart) Social Network Sites: The Role of Networked Publics in Teenage Social Life," MacArthur Foundation Series on Digital Learning—Youth, Identity, and Digital Media Volume, ed. David Buckingham (Cambridge MA: MIT Press, 2007).

6. Erik Erikson, *Identity and the Life Cycle* (Madison CT: International Universities Press, 1959); Abraham Maslow, *Motivation and Personality* (New York: Harper Press, 1954).

7. boyd, "Why Youth (Heart) Social Network Sites."

8. Christian Smith, *Soul Searching: The Religious and Spiritual Lives of American Teenagers* (New York: Oxford Press, 2005) 162ff.

9. Ibid., 220.

10. Erving Goffman, *The Presentation of Self in Everyday Life* (Garden City NY: Doubleday, 1959) 2.

11. Anne Lamott, *Traveling Mercies: Some Thoughts on Faith* (New York: Pantheon, 1999).

12. Mike Yaconelli, *Messy Spirituality* (Grand Rapids MI: Zondervan, 2002) 121.

13. Heather Horst, *Hanging Out, Messing Around, and Geeking Out: Kids Living and Learning with New Media*, ed. Mizuko Ito (Cambridge MA: MIT, 2010) 164.

14. David Kinnaman, *You Lost Me* (Grand Rapids MI: Baker, 2011) 59–88.

15. Christian Smith and Melissa Lundquist Denton, *Soul Searching: the Religious and Spiritual Lives of American Teenagers* (New York: Oxford, 2005) 266.

16. Ibid., 77.

17. Robin Dunbar, "Coevolution of Neocortical Size, Group Size and Language in Humans," *Behavioral and Brain Sciences* 16/4 (1993): 691.

18. Carl Bialik, "Sorry, You May Have Gone Over Your Limit of Network Friends," *Wall Street Journal*, 16 November 2007, http://online.wsj.com/news/articles/SB119518271549595364 (accessed 7 February 2014).

19. Peter Block, podcast, "Community: The Structure of Belonging," Seeking Community, 2012, http://seekingcommunity.ca/content/peter-block-community-structure-belonging#1 (accessed 1 March 2013).

20. American Idol statistics, 2012, http://www.foxnews.com/entertainment/2012/05/23/american-idol-crowns-season-11-winner/ (accessed 3 March 2013).

21. New York: Basic Books, 2011.

22. Brian Foreman, blog post, "From Hi-Tech to High Touch: Connections and Community," 19 March 2013, http://socialmediaparents.com/from-hi-tech-to-high-touch-affirmations-social-media-parents/ (accessed 7 February 2014).

23. Jane McGonical, February 2011, http://www.ted.com/conversations/44/we_spend_3_billion_hours_a_wee.html (accessed 7 February 2014).

24. "Facebook 2012," Infographic Labs, February 2012, http://infographiclabs.com/news/facebook-2012 (accessed 11 August 2012).

25. Craig Malkin, quoted in Andrea Shea, "Facebook Envy: How the Social Network Affects Our Self-esteem," 90.9wbur, 20 February 2013, http://www.wbur.org/2013/02/20/facebook-perfection (accessed 5 March 2013).

26. Stanley Hauerwaus and William H. Willimon, *Resident Aliens* (Nashville: Abingdon Press, 1989).

27. Ibid., 12–13; 43–49.

28. Common Sense, "Social Media, Social Life."

29. Boyd, "Why Youth (Heart) Social Network Sites."

Appendix

Glossary of Social Media Terms, Applications, and Platforms

Application (app): Applications are software that allows digital devices to function. You might remember these being called *programs.* Hundreds of thousands of apps exist for smartphones and tablets that allow users access to social media platforms, games, productivity tools, and more. Many social media platforms have specifically designed apps for their users.

Blog: A blog is a web- or Internet-based writing tool where users publish information that is sometimes discussion-oriented and other times just informational. Most blog posts are 300–500 words. The blog may be tied to an individual, an organization, or a business.

Facebook: The largest of the social media platforms, Facebook allows users to share pictures, thoughts, opinions, and Internet links with those with whom they are connected, commonly known on the site as their *friends.*

Foursquare: This GPS-based location application allows users to "check-in" at locations on their smartphones, gaining information (tips, advice, opinions) about their whereabouts and others who may be checked in as well. Foursquare allows you to share about the places you visit and post your own recommendations as well.

Friend: A *friend* in the social media world means something different from what we intend in real life. A *friend* is generally someone to whom you are connected through a social media platform. Some platforms use the term *followers* instead of *friends. Followers* and *friends* differ in that *follower* implies a one-way connection, whereas a friend connection is two-way (i.e., two people connected to one another).

Google: Aside from being the largest search engine in the world, Google also has its own social media platform, Google+, as well as a bevy of additional web-based applications, like Maps, Books, and Docs. Social sharing is becoming more integrated with Google searches, where recommendations from people with whom you are friends show up in your search if there is relevant data to share.

Hashtag: The "#" sign is primarily affixed to social media posts to designate a search category under which related posts can be found. This is a key feature in Twitter that allows searches based on hashtags. For instance, if you want to follow the online banter during a major sporting event, one only has to follow the assigned hashtag for that event (e.g., #SuperBowlXLVIII).

A second use of the hashtag has originated that allows the post creator to add a snarky, sarcastic, or editorial comment to their post. For example, *#sorrynotsorry* lets you know the poster is clearly not as apologetic as the print preceding the hashtag might otherwise indicate.

Instagram: This is a photo-sharing web-based social media platform that allows users to post pictures, employing a variety of photo effect lenses, about which followers can post comments or simply "like" the picture.

Like: All social media platforms seek to create interaction or engagement. The simplest form of that is to "like" someone's post. In Facebook there is a "Like" button. Twitter offers a "Favorite" star. Almost all major platforms have some form of feedback button based on the principle of "liking" the post.

LinkedIn: To date, LinkedIn has been used as a professional social media platform that allows users to search for professional connections among their personal connections. LinkedIn also allows the user to have a profile that reads like a resume, post information or articles of interest in their field, and connect through professional discussion groups within the LinkedIn platform. Not generally used by teenagers, LinkedIn was still the fastest-growing social media platform in 2013.

Meetup: This event planning and organizing platform allows users to find connections and events in which they might like to participate, generally based on location and personal interest. Groups are created, and a user can join those groups and receive regular updates about upcoming events and other members.

Path: This social media platform is based on Dunbar's number, the theory that a person can only have a finite number of meaningful relationships and friends. Path limits user "friends" to 150, and tends to encourage more personal sharing. Path functions much like Facebook in every other regard for sharing status updates, photos, and location information.

Pinterest: Imagine a room filled with countless corkboards, each designated to contain information about a specific topic. Pinterest is a digital version of that. Users can "pin" articles and pictures, among other things, to their chosen boards for later reference. By following other users and some of their boards, users can re-pin information they want to keep handy for themselves.

Platform: This is a term commonly given to reference the multitude of social media networks that allows users to connect, interact, and share information. Each platform allows this connectivity through either a web-based application, a mobile app, or both.

Post: A post refers to information that users place on their social media platforms. Posts range from commentary to blog entries to pictures and videos, to, well, you name it. If it can be shared digitally, it becomes a post.

Share: An original post created, information reposted, and sending a link are all forms of sharing. Most news outlets now even provide means by which to share an article directly from their websites through social media platforms. Sharing and resharing is what creates a post that goes viral. When an item goes viral, it is usually an organic process that happens because people are compelled by content to reshare the post.

Snapchat: This photo-sharing platform burst onto the scene as a means to send photos which disappeared after a few seconds, and could not be saved by the sender or receiver. Snapchat also allows user to write on top of the photos, creating a fun environment for users to send silly photos to one another.

Tag: To tag something or someone means to include a person's name with a post so that they receive notification about it or so that they are identifiable in the picture. For example, on Facebook users can tag people in their photos, thus allowing those who are tagged to save or have access to the photos as well. Often tags are also used to draw another user's attention to a post.

Text (texting): Sending a text, or texting, is a more frequent form a communication for adolescents on their phones than actually placing a phone call. Short messages are typed and sent through the phone's data plan. Photos, videos, and web links can also be sent through most messaging services now.

Tweet (tweeting): A tweet is post on Twitter. These micro-blog posts are limited to 140 characters and can include text, links, video, photos, and more. Tweets show up in the Twitter streams (Timeline) of the poster's followers. More specific tweets can be addressed to other users through a direct message (hidden between users who mutually follow one another), or by including another user's Twitter name, referred to as their handle, and designated with a "@" sign attached at the beginning (e.g., my Twitter handle is @b4man72).

Twitter: This social media platform is a 140 character micro-blogging platform that allows users to compose short messages that are broadcast through Twitter's timeline. These tweets show up in the timelines of the original poster's followers. Twitter is emerging as a powerful tool for connecting with others, marketing brands, and garnering instant information and reaction to events.

Viggle: This social media application is tied directly to your television-watching habits. Viggle users can interact with others in real time who are all watching the same television shows together. Networks and advertisers alike are able to create interactive experiences with viewers.

Wii (and **Wii U**): While Sony has the PlayStation and Microsoft the Xbox, Nintendo has the Wii. These video game systems are a far cry from the Atari 2600 I played as a child. These are full entertainment devices that play games, videos, access the Internet, and allow for social media sharing through the games. Many adults do not consider the ability of children and teens to access, and *be accessed by*, other gamers around the world.

Sample Contract for a Family's Social Media Use

This is a sample contract to help you get started. Remember to use language that works for your family. If "contract" sounds too legalistic, change it.

What Being Online Means

Being online is time that you spend texting, tweeting, and using Facebook. We expect you to be online at appropriate times (after 11:00 pm and during class are examples of inappropriate times). We expect you to be engaged with us when we are at meals or having other family times.

As you join new networks, we expect you to let us know where you are engaging. We may or may not set up an account, but we do want to know.

Current Platforms:_____

Online Interaction

1. We will monitor your posts on the social media platforms where you participate.
2. We will not comment publicly or embarrass you through them.
3. If we are too actively involved with you, please let us know and we will adjust.
4. We will not send messages or requests to your friends, but if they invite us, we will accept their requests.
5. Since you have requested that we not comment on Facebook, we will simply be aware of what you are posting with occasional check-ins.

Safety

Your safety is one of our primary concerns, not just online but throughout life in general. While we trust you to make good decisions, we still want to be certain that we are doing our jobs as your parents.

1. As a family, our privacy settings are limited to friends and family. Location-based apps that are open to the public allow too many people to see who you are and where you are, and to call you by name.
2. When we see things that concern us, we will come to you to discuss it. If we ask you to take something down and you don't understand, we expect

you to honor our request. We will do our best to explain why we are asking you to do so. You are welcome to explain if you think we are over-reacting, and while we may change our minds, the final decision will still be ours.

3. We expect you to discuss with us if someone is making you feel uncomfortable online, whether it is bullying from other teens or strangers making contact with you. We cannot help you unless you allow us to, and we greatly desire to do so.

Privacy

Privacy matters to us. Yours is important, and we want to respect it. But safety is still a major concern. If you ever feel that we are invading your privacy, we ask that you tell us so we can discuss it.

1. A log of your accounts and passwords is to be kept for us. We will keep it safe from your siblings, as we know that you do not want your older brother to post Facebook updates on your account.

2. Random scans will be made on your accounts. You are a part of this process, so you will be with us when we conduct them. Nothing is being done behind your back.

3. During the scans, we will look for these things:

   a. followers or friends that concern us.

   b. that your privacy settings are where we expect them to be.

   c. if there is anything that concerns us and merits a discussion with you.

Where You Use Social Media

There are times when using your phone is not appropriate. For example, please don't text or take pictures during the worship service at church. Your grandma does not understand Twitter, so please save your tweets for when she is not watching you.

Please be aware that not all parents like having their teens tagged in photos and locations. Know what your friends' parents expect so that you don't get in trouble with them for tagging a photo. We know that your friend can remove the tag, and we hope they will, but awareness is good on your part.

Decorum

1. Bullying in any shape or form is never allowed. You will face serious consequences if we determine that you are participating in such behavior. Zero-tolerance policy!

2. There are topics that we as a family will not discuss in social media. These include family conflicts. You can be mad at your brother and say so online, but do not enlist people in the argument. Other topics include family money, gossip, or private situations. If you are not sure about sharing, don't share.

Addressing Concerns

The things listed below are major concerns. If we see something like this, we will start with a conversation with you.
1. Bullying behavior (conducting it, condoning it, being a victim of it)
2. Self-destructive behavior (by you or your friends)
3. Inappropriate connections and conversations with them (you are fourteen years old and should not be chatting with a thirty-year-old man)
4. Drug or alcohol use
5. Sexual harassment (conducting or victimized by it)

Every year, at the start of school, we will review and revise this contract. If unseen issues arise, we will discuss them and renegotiate the contract as necessary.

Signature:_____

Signature:_____

Other available titles from

#Connect
Reaching Youth Across the Digital Divide
Brian Foreman

Reaching our youth across the digital divide is a struggle for parents, ministers, and other adults who work with Generation Z— today's teenagers. *#Connect* leads readers into the technological landscape, encourages conversations with teenagers, and reminds us all to be the presence of Christ in every facet of our lives. *978-1-57312-693-9 120 pages/pb* **$13.00**

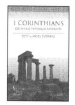

1 Corinthians (Smyth & Helwys Annual Bible Study series)
Growing through Diversity
Don & Anita Flowers

Don and Anita Flowers present this comprehensive study of 1 Corinthians, filled with scholarly insight and dealing with such varied topics as marriage and sexuality, spiritual gifts and love, and diversity and unity. The authors examine Paul's relationship with the church in Corinth as well as the culture of that city to give context to topics that can seem far removed from Christian life today. *Teaching Guide 978-1-57312-701-1 122 pages/pb* **$14.00**
Study Guide 978-1-57312-705-9 52 pages/pb **$6.00**

Beyond the American Dream
Millard Fuller

In 1968, Millard finished the story of his journey from pauper to millionaire to home builder. His wife, Linda, occasionally would ask him about getting it published, but Millard would reply, "Not now. I'm too busy." This is that story. *978-1-57312-563-5 272 pages/pb* **$20.00**

Blissful Affliction
The Ministry and Misery of Writing
Judson Edwards

Edwards draws from more than forty years of writing experience to explore why we use the written word to change lives and how to improve the writing craft. *978-1-57312-594-9 144 pages/pb* **$15.00**

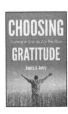

Choosing Gratitude
Learning to Love the Life You Have

James A. Autry

Autry reminds us that gratitude is a choice, a spiritual—not social—process. He suggests that if we cultivate gratitude as a way of being, we may not change the world and its ills, but we can change our response to the world. If we fill our lives with moments of gratitude, we will indeed love the life we have. 978-1-57312-614-4 *144 pages/pb* **$15.00**

Choosing Gratitude 365 Days a Year
Your Daily Guide to Grateful Living

James A. Autry and Sally J. Pederson

Filled with quotes, poems, and the inspired voices of both Pederson and Autry, in a society consumed by fears of not having "enough"— money, possessions, security, and so on—this book suggests that if we cultivate gratitude as a way of being, we may not change the world and its ills, but we can change our response to the world. 978-1-57312-689-2 *210 pages/pb* **$18.00**

Contextualizing the Gospel
A Homiletic Commentary on 1 Corinthians

Brian L. Harbour

Harbour examines every part of Paul's letter, providing a rich resource for those who want to struggle with the difficult texts as well as the simple texts, who want to know how God's word—all of it—intersects with their lives today. 978-1-57312-589-5 *240 pages/pb* **$19.00**

Dance Lessons
Moving to the Beat of God's Heart

Jeanie Miley

Miley shares her joys and struggles a she learns to "dance" with the Spirit of the Living God. 978-1-57312-622-9 *240 pages/pb* **$19.00**

A Divine Duet
Ministry and Motherhood

Alicia Davis Porterfield, ed.

Each essay in this inspiring collection is as different as the mother-minister who wrote it, from theologians to chaplains, inner-city ministers to rural-poverty ministers, youth pastors to preachers, mothers who have adopted, birthed, and done both.

978-1-57312-676-2 *146 pages/pb* **$16.00**

The Enoch Factor
The Sacred Art of Knowing God

Steve McSwain

The Enoch Factor is a persuasive argument for a more enlightened religious dialogue in America, one that affirms the goals of all religions—guiding followers in self-awareness, finding serenity and happiness, and discovering what the author describes as "the sacred art of knowing God."

978-1-57312-556-7 *256 pages/pb* **$21.00**

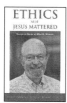

Ethics as if Jesus Mattered
Essays in Honor of Glen H. Stassen

Rick Axtell, Michelle Tooley, Michael L. Westmoreland-White, eds.

Ethics as if Jesus Mattered will introduce Stassen's work to a new generation, advance dialogue and debate in Christian ethics, and inspire more faithful discipleship just as it honors one whom the contributors consider a mentor.

978-1-57312-695-3 *234 pages/pb* **$18.00**

Healing Our Hurts
Coping with Difficult Emotions

Daniel Bagby

In *Healing Our Hurts*, Daniel Bagby identifies and explains all the dynamics at play in these complex emotions. Offering practical biblical insights to these feelings, he interprets faith-based responses to separate overly religious piety from true, natural human emotion. This book helps us learn how to deal with life's difficult emotions in a redemptive and responsible way.

978-1-57312-613-7 *144 pages/pb* **$15.00**

Help! I Teach Youth Sunday School

Brian Foreman, Bo Prosser, and David Woody

Real-life stories are mingled with information on Youth and their culture, common myths about Sunday School, a new way of preparing the Sunday school lesson, creative teaching ideas, ways to think about growing a class, and how to reach out for new members and reach in to old members.

1-57312-427-3 *128 pages/pb* **$14.0**

Hope for the Thinking Christian
Seeking a Path of Faith through Everyday Life

Stephen Reese

Readers who want to confront their faith more directly, to think it through and be open to God in an individual, authentic, spiritual encounter will find a resonant voice in Stephen Reese.

978-1-57312-553-6 *160 pages/pb* **$16.00**

To order call **1-800-747-3016** or visit **www.helwys.com**

A Hungry Soul Desperate to Taste God's Grace
Honest Prayers for Life

Charles Qualls

Part of how we *see* God is determined by how we *listen* to God. There is so much noise and movement in the world that competes with images of God. This noise would drown out God's beckoning voice and distract us. Charles Qualls's newest book offers readers prayers for that journey toward the meaning and mystery of God.   *978-1-57312-648-9 152 pages/pb* **$14.00**

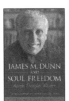

James M. Dunn and Soul Freedom

Aaron Douglas Weaver

James Milton Dunn, over the last fifty years, has been the most aggressive Baptist proponent for religious liberty in the United States. Soul freedom—voluntary, uncoerced faith and an unfettered individual conscience before God—is the basis of his understanding of church-state separation and the historic Baptist basis of religious liberty.   *978-1-57312-590-1 224 pages/pb* **$18.00**

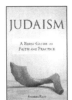

The Jesus Tribe
Following Christ in the Land of the Empire

Ronnie McBrayer

The Jesus Tribe fleshes out the implications, possibilities, contradictions, and complexities of what it means to live within the Jesus Tribe and in the shadow of the American Empire.

978-1-57312-592-5 208 pages/pb **$17.00**

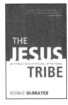

Judaism
A Brief Guide to Faith and Practice

Sharon Pace

Sharon Pace's newest book is a sensitive and comprehensive introduction to Judaism. What is it like to be born into the Jewish community? How does belief in the One God and a universal morality shape the way in which Jews see the world? How does one find meaning in life and the courage to endure suffering? How does one mark joy and forge community ties?   *978-1-57312-644-1 144 pages/pb* **$16.00**

Lessons from the Cloth 2
501 More One Minute Motivators for Leaders

Bo Prosser and Charles Qualls

As the force that drives organizations to accomplishment, leadership is at a crucial point in churches, corporations, families, and almost every arena of life. In this follow-up to their first volume, Prosser and Qualls will inspire you to keep growing in your leadership career.

978-1-57312-665-6 152 pages/pb **$11.00**

Let Me More of Their Beauty See
Reading Familiar Verses in Context
Diane G. Chen

Let Me More of Their Beauty See offers eight examples of how attention to the historical and literary settings can safeguard against taking a text out of context, bring out its transforming power in greater dimension, and help us apply Scripture appropriately in our daily lives.

978-1-57312-564-2 160 pages/pb **$17.00**

Looking Around for God
The Strangely Reverent Observations of an Unconventional Christian
James A. Autry

Looking Around for God, Autry's tenth book, is in many ways his most personal. In it he considers his unique life of faith and belief in God. Autry is a former Fortune 500 executive, author, poet, and consultant whose work has had a significant influence on leadership thinking.

978-157312-484-3 144 pages/pb **$16.00**

Making the Timeless Word Timely
A Primer for Preachers
Michael B. Brown

Michael Brown writes, "There is a simple formula for sermon preparation that creates messages that apply and engage whether your parish is rural or urban, young or old, rich or poor, five thousand members or fifty." The other part of the task, of course, involves being creative and insightful enough to know how to take the general formula for sermon preparation and make it particular in its impact on a specific congregation. Brown guides the reader through the formula and the skills to employ it with excellence and integrity.

978-1-57312-578-9 160 pages/pb **$16.00**

Meeting Jesus Today
For the Cautious, the Curious, and the Committed
Jeanie Miley

Meeting Jesus Today, ideal for both individual study and small groups, is intended to be used as a workbook. It is designed to move readers from studying the Scriptures and ideas within the chapters to recording their journey with the Living Christ.

978-1-57312-677-9 320 pages/pb **$19.00**

The Ministry Life
101 Tips for New Ministers
John Killinger

Sharing years of wisdom from more than fifty years in ministry and teaching, *The Ministry Life: 101 Tips for New Ministers* by John Killinger is filled with practical advice and wisdom for a minister's day-to-day tasks as well as advice on intellectual and spiritual habits to keep ministers of any age healthy and fulfilled. *978-1-57312-662-5 244 pages/pb* **$19.00**

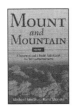

Mount and Mountain
Vol. 1: A Reverend and a Rabbi Talk About the Ten Commandments
Rami Shapiro and Michael Smith

Mount and Mountain represents the first half of an interfaith dialogue—a dialogue that neither preaches nor placates but challenges its participants to work both singly and together in the task of reinterpreting sacred texts. Mike and Rami discuss the nature of divinity, the power of faith, the beauty of myth and story, the necessity of doubt, the achievements, failings, and future of religion, and, above all, the struggle to live ethically and in harmony with the way of God. *978-1-57312-612-0 144 pages/pb* **$15.00**

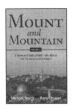

Mount and Mountain
Vol. 2: A Reverend and a Rabbi Talk About the Sermon on the Mount
Rami Shapiro and Michael Smith

This book, focused on the Sermon on the Mount, represents the second half of Mike and Rami's dialogue. In it, Mike and Rami explore the text of Jesus' sermon cooperatively, contributing perspectives drawn from their lives and religious traditions and seeking moments of illumination. *978-1-57312-654-0 254 pages/pb* **$19.00**

Overcoming Adolescence
Growing Beyond Childhood into Maturity
Marion D. Aldridge

In *Overcoming Adolescence*, Marion D. Aldridge poses questions for adults of all ages to consider. His challenge to readers is one he has personally worked to confront: to grow up *all the way*—mentally, physically, academically, socially, emotionally, and spiritually. The key involves not only knowing how to work through the process but also how to recognize what may be contributing to our perpetual adolescence.

978-1-57312-577-2 156 pages/pb **$17.00**

Psychic Pancakes & Communion Pizza
More Musings and Mutterings of a Church Misfit

Bert Montgomery

Psychic Pancakes & Communion Pizza is Bert Montgomery's highly anticipated follow-up to *Elvis, Willie, Jesus & Me* and contains further reflections on music, film, culture, life, and finding Jesus in the midst of it all. *978-1-57312-578-9 160 pages/pb* **$16.00**

Quiet Faith
An Introvert's Guide to Spiritual Survival

Judson Edwards

In eight finely crafted chapters, Edwards looks at key issues like evangelism, interpreting the Bible, dealing with doubt, and surviving the church from the perspective of a confirmed, but sometimes reluctant, introvert. In the process, he offers some provocative insights that introverts will find helpful and reassuring. *978-1-57312-681-6 144 pages/pb* **$15.00**

Reading Ezekiel (Reading the Old Testament series)
A Literary and Theological Commentary

Marvin A. Sweeney

The book of Ezekiel points to the return of YHWH to the holy temple at the center of a reconstituted Israel and creation at large. As such, the book of Ezekiel portrays the purging of Jerusalem, the Temple, and the people, to reconstitute them as part of a new creation at the conclusion of the book. With Jerusalem, the Temple, and the people so purged, YHWH stands once again in the holy center of the created world.

978-1-57312-658-8 264 pages/pb **$22.00**

Reading Hosea–Micah
(Reading the Old Testament series)
A Literary and Theological Commentary

Terence E. Fretheim

Terence E. Fretheim explores themes of indictment, judgment, and salvation in Hosea–Micah. The indictment against the people of God especially involves issues of idolatry, as well as abuse of the poor and needy. The effects of such behaviors are often horrendous in their severity. While God is often the subject of such judgments, the consequences, like fruit, grow out of the deed itself. *978-1-57312-687-8 224 pages/pb* **$22.00**

Reading Samuel (Reading the Old Testament series)
A Literary and Theological Commentary
Johanna W. H. van Wijk-Bos

Interpreted masterfully by preeminent Old Testament scholar Johanna W. H. van Wijk-Bos, the story of Samuel touches on a vast array of subjects that make up the rich fabric of human life. The reader gains an inside look at leadership, royal intrigue, military campaigns, occult practices, and the significance of religious objects of veneration.

978-1-57312-607-6 272 pages/pb **$22.00**

Sessions with Genesis (Session Bible Studies series)
The Story Begins
Tony W. Cartledge

Immersing us in the book of Genesis, Tony W. Cartledge examines both its major stories and the smaller cycles of hope and failure, of promise and judgment. Genesis introduces these themes of divine faithfulness and human failure in unmistakable terms, tracing Israel's beginning to the creation of the world and professing a belief that Israel's particular history had universal significance.

978-1-57312-636-6 144 pages/pb **$14.00**

Sessions with Revelation (Session Bible Studies series)
The Final Days of Evil
David Sapp

David Sapp's careful guide through Revelation demonstrates that it is a letter of hope for believers; it is less about the last days of history than it is about the last days of evil. Without eliminating its mystery, Sapp unlocks Revelation's central truths so that its relevance becomes clear.

978-1-57312-706-6 166 pages/pb **$14.00**

Silver Linings
My Life Before and After *Challenger 7*
June Scobee Rodgers

We know the public story of *Challenger 7*'s tragic destruction. That day, June's life took a new direction that ultimately led to the creation of the Challenger Center and to new life and new love. Her story of Christian faith and triumph over adversity will inspire readers of every age.

978-1-57312-570-3 352 pages/hc **$28.00**

978-1-57312-694-6 352 pages/pb **$18.00**

Spacious
Exploring Faith and Place
Holly Sprink

Exploring where we are and why that matters to God is an ongoing process. If we are present and attentive, God creatively and continuously widens our view of the world.   *978-1-57312-649-6 156 pages/pb* **$16.00**

The Teaching Church
Congregation as Mentor
Christopher M. Hamlin / Sarah Jackson Shelton

Collected in *The Teaching Church: Congregation as Mentor* are the stories of the pastors who shared how congregations have shaped, nurtured, and, sometimes, broken their resolve to be faithful servants of God.   *978-1-57312-682-3 112 pages/pb* **$13.00**

A Time to Laugh
Humor in the Bible
Mark E. Biddle

An extension of his well-loved seminary course on humor in the Bible, *A Time to Laugh* draws on Mark E. Biddle's command of Hebrew language and cultural subtleties to explore the ways humor was intentionally incorporated into Scripture. With characteristic liveliness, Biddle guides the reader through the stories of six biblical characters who did rather unexpected things.   *978-1-57312-683-0 164 pages/pb* **$14.00**

This Is What a Preacher Looks Like
Sermons by Baptist Women in Ministry
Pamela Durso, ed.

In this collection of sermons by thirty-six Baptist women, their voices are soft and loud, prophetic and pastoral, humorous and sincere. They are African American, Asian, Latina, and Caucasian. They are sisters, wives, mothers, grandmothers, aunts, and friends.

978-1-57312-554-3 144 pages/pb **$18.00**

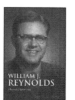

William J. Reynolds
Church Musician
David W. Music

William J. Reynolds is renowned among Baptist musicians, music ministers, song leaders, and hymnody students. In eminently readable style, David W. Music's comprehensive biography describes Reynolds's family and educational background, his career as a minister of music, denominational leader, and seminary professor.   *978-1-57312-690-8 358 pages/pb* **$23.00**

Made in the USA
San Bernardino, CA
27 May 2014